BACKYARD FARMING
Modern Techniques for Self-Sufficiency on Less Than an Acre

CODY TRENT

Introduction

Years ago, I stood in my backyard, staring at a patch of scraggly grass and a few stubborn weeds. I dreamed of turning that small, uninspiring space into a thriving oasis of food and self-sufficiency. It wasn't a smooth journey. There were late research nights, early labour mornings, and a fair share of failures. But each plant that took root, each harvest that filled our table, transformed our backyard and lives. That small plot of land gave us more than food; it gave us a sense of accomplishment and a deeper connection to the earth.

The purpose of this book is to share that journey with you. I want to empower you to achieve self-sufficiency using modern backyard farming techniques, even if you have less than an acre. You don't need a sprawling farm to grow food and raise chickens. You can turn even the smallest yard into a productive homestead with the proper techniques and dedication.

We'll cover a wide range of topics to get you started. You'll learn about outdoor gardening, including how to make the most of your space and grow various vegetables. We'll dive into the benefits of greenhouses and hoop houses, which can extend your growing season and protect your plants. For those interested in more advanced techniques, we'll explore hydroponics and effective water management. We'll also discuss the importance of plant nutrients, guiding you on how to keep your soil healthy and your plants thriving.

Timing is crucial in gardening, so you'll find detailed chapters on the best planting and harvest times for different vegetables. We'll discuss crop proportions and sizing to help you plan your garden efficiently. And, of course, we can't forget the importance of selecting and saving seeds, ensuring you have a sustainable garden year after year. Lastly, we'll touch on raising chickens and providing fresh eggs and natural fertilizer for your garden.

Why is all this important? There's a growing interest in self-sufficiency and sustainable living. More people recognize the benefits of growing their food and reducing their reliance on commercial systems. Homeowners, urban dwellers, and new homesteaders alike seek ways to make the most of their limited space. This book is for anyone who wants to take control of their food supply and live more sustainably.

Allow me to introduce myself. I'm Cody Trent, and I am passionate about helping people overcome limited space challenges. I've spent years gardening and homesteading and learned a lot. I aim to share that knowledge with you in a way that's easy to understand and apply. I believe anyone can achieve self-sufficiency, no matter the size of their yard.

Your journey will begin with planning your homestead. We'll look at how to assess your space and decide what to grow. From there, we'll move on to planting and caring for your crops. You'll learn about different gardening techniques and how to adapt them to your space. As you start to see the fruits of your labour, we'll talk about harvesting and preserving your bounty, ensuring you can enjoy your homegrown food all year round.

I encourage you to embrace the techniques and practices detailed in this book. It might seem daunting initially, but I promise it's rewarding. There's nothing quite like the taste of a vegetable you've grown yourself or the satisfaction of knowing you're providing for your family. So roll up your sleeves, grab your gardening tools, and let's get started. Together, we'll turn your backyard into a productive, self-sufficient homestead.

Table of Contents

CHAPTER 1 LAYING THE GROUNDWORK

I was on my porch with tea, and my lawn was unattended, drinking tea and watching the dusk. I knew then that the little parcel of land with so much potential for use had been ignored for some time. This was my first step after yard care to a community of sustainable, self-sufficient land. It allowed me to pick up control of my life, which urban life had swallowed up; it meant that it began to become more than simply gardening to develop edible plants in this space. Tcaching core self-sufficiency principles and their significant effects is the groundwork of your transformational process.

1.1 Understanding Self-Sufficiency and Its Benefits

Self-sufficiency goes beyond marketing jargon because it gives individuals food source authority while decreasing commercial dependence and building sustainability. The trend of convenient living has allowed most people to lose control over their food staples, but caring for your food patches helps you reestablish this authority. The cultivation of vegetables and fruits, together with backyard chicken rearing, allows you to slash your grocery expenses considerably. Entering your backyard will enable you to harvest fresh tomatoes alongside lettuce and herbs, which you can use for your salad instead of purchasing them at the store. Although the initial costs appear costly, the savings build up gradually, thus making the investment profitable in the long run.

Control over your food production guarantees independence from food prices and the safety of your nutritious food supply. Knowledge of food origins combined with understanding the farming processes gives you comfort. Increasing food production becomes crucial because it provides fresh and healthy eating while eliminating any risks from harmful chemicals, often happening during food safety scares at large food production companies. Managing your food supply directly represents an invaluable asset, especially during rising uncertainties.

Backyard farming generates multiple environmental rewards alongside its other benefits. The traditional farming sector and extensive grocery shipment operations produce high levels of greenhouse gases from fossil fuel use. Home food cultivation creates a smaller carbon footprint and supports future sustainability goals. Your health and environmental sustainability improve because organic gardening eliminates dangerous pesticides and fertilizers from your operation. Vegetable waste and garden materials become high-quality compost when combined for composting purposes; thus, your waste creates a natural recycling cycle for your soil.

Backyard farming creates extensive physical and mental health advantages—gardening triggers stress reduction and better mental well-being outcomes. Growing your garden while brushing soil between your fingers provides healing effects, which are both physical and mental. Physical exercise is a significant advantage among the many benefits of backyard farming. Physical effort that involves digging, planting, weeding, and doing other backyard farming activities hand-in-hand with harvesting helps to improve cardiovascular health and build strength of muscles while improving flexibility. A way to escape our busy modern world is to spend time outside and connect with nature, creating tranquillity and a connection to the land.

Backyard farming enables people to achieve personal satisfaction while feeling accomplished. Having control over your food production brings you deep satisfaction. The entire harvest reflects the physical effort you dedicated to growing it. Your self-pride reaches its peak when you provide a dinner prepared using vegetables you grew yourself. Beyond food production, the sense of being self-sufficient leads to developing an attitude for personal strength, which spreads across various areas of your existence.

The Dervaes family successfully operated their urban homestead known as "Path to Freedom" on a suburban property in Pasadena, California. This operation generates over 6,000 pounds yearly from a total acreage of one-tcnth. The homeowners use vertical gardening and raised beds with composting systems while keeping chickens and ducks together with rabbits and goats on their farm. The Dervaes family uses their garden space to sustain their household needs while exporting fresh produce to high-end restaurants and caterers, proving that harmful investments in tiny acreage can produce exceptional outcomes.

Jules Dervaes and his children established an urban homestead that became a self-sufficient example for urban dwellers. Installing a 2 kW solar power system enables the company to become a self-sufficient oasis as it cuts its dependence on outside energy suppliers. Their sustainability practice includes brown water recycling and waste vegetable oil conservation for biodiesel fuel production while focusing on minimal water consumption. The experience demonstrates that self-sufficiency extends beyond food production, including energy distribution, treatment, and water supply.

Suburban backyard farmers have also become self-sufficient. In Sa-rah's case, for example, a mother of one who begins to grow her vegetables to save on groceries. That could be a cost-saving side; it became a passion. It was a joy to a garden, and it improved her physical health and brought her closer to her community by giving her crop away in exchange for free labour. Sarah's story explains that one person alone can influence self-sufficiency, not only with themselves but with their family and neighbourhood.

It's a movement toward a more sustainable and fulfilling way of living, not just a fad. Backyard farming helps you become healthier and self-reliant, contributing to a more sustainable future. If you're a novice homesteader, a homeowner, or an urbanite with a little patio to learn from, I hope you find this book easy to read and helpful. It provides the skills and inspiration you need to transform your backyard into a self-sufficient homestead, from basic self-sufficiency to sophisticated, contemporary gardening techniques.

1.2 Planning Your Backyard Homestead: Space, Budget, and Time Management

For my trans-form, I knew someone was going to have to plan. The first step is to assess the workable space in your backyard farm layout. Firstly, it works by measuring and mapping the area to be worked on. Measure your yard using a tape measure, and create a crude map. It will allow you to picture how much space you can dedicate to each function: garden beds, chicken coop, or whatever else that is vital for you to function as a homesteader, even if on a small scale. It is essential to be precise because each square foot counts.

For this reason, zoning different functional areas is necessary to maximize productivity. Consider how you can section off your area into zones. For instance, the chicken coop needs solid shade because the hens are too hot; however, your garden beds are under the sun. Alleys should be wide enough to make getting around as easy as possible yet not so grandiose as to squander precious growing space. Don't forget the vertical dimension. Trellises and wall-mounted planters are verticle gardening solutions that help you grow more in less space. Another great option for container gardening is patios and balconies, where every inch of space counts.

Though budgeting for your backyard homestead can seem daunting, it is manageable when you break it down. These initial costs include seeds, tools, and materials for raised beds or containers. Seeds are cheap; tools can add up, too, such as spades, hoes, and watering cans. Cutting corners by utilizing second-hand tools at garage sales or online marketplaces. Raised beds can be made of reclaimed wood or other inexpensive materials. Expenses that continue once the garden is constructed include soil amendments, water usage, and the cost of possible pest control. DIY alternatives to expensive offers are the way to keep costs down. For example, a compost bin can be made from old pallets, or a simple drip irrigation can be built from plastic tubing and a few connectors.

If you are living a busy life, then managing your time is essential. To begin with, make a weekly and daily task schedule. It is first noted which tasks should be completed daily, like watering or looking for pests, and which can be done weekly, such as weeding or harvesting. In your gardening, there are some time-saving techniques. Mulching your garden beds lessens the amount of watering and weeding that is needed. Automation tools like drip irrigation systems can also lend a helping hand by automating the task of proper watering without you doing it manually. If you have family members and housemates, divide the task and distribute it to all. Young children can even do simple tasks such as watering or collecting eggs.

The secret to all this is not to set unrealistic goals and expectations so you won't be frustrated and burned out. Start by prioritizing key projects. Please do not attempt to do it all at once. Growing as a greenie means building one or two main projects, such as raising beds or a chicken co-op, and growing as growth occurs. One of the first things is to manage expectations for the first year. Know that not everything will be perfect, and that is okay. Know where you stand and enjoy the small wins. Maintaining a garden journal allows you to write down what's working — and what's not — so you can later make informed changes based on implementing your new ground cover ideas and feedback from each expanding year.

One thing that helps is creating a checklist of short-term and long-term goals. For example, short-term objectives could be planting your first batch of seeds or installing a simple compost bin. Expanding your garden beds or installing a greenhouse are two long-term goals. Having these goals to begin with helps you focus and keeps you motivated. No matter how small your achievement, celebrate it. Every step is progress in the direction of a more self-sufficient lifestyle.

By incorporating these planning strategies, you can use your available space most, keep within your budget, and manage your time correctly. This is another tactic to plan out everything carefully, and then you will be well on your way to success and build that productive, sustainable backyard homestead. Why not achieve a balance or a maximum of what you have—a big yard or only five square meters of the balcony? Thoughtful planning can turn any space into a thriving homestead that produces fresh food and invigorates you.

CHAPTER 2 SOIL AND COM-
POSTING BASICS

The soil forms the basis of any successful garden. I remember the first time I sunk my fingers into the earth as I
hoped, but instead found complex, hard-packed clay. It was
disheartening, but I learned what soil health means and why
in a productive garden. This first step is crucial because the
quality of your soil makes (or breaks) all of your efforts to
transform your backyard into a thriving homestead.

2.1 Assessing and Improving Soil Quality

What kind of soil are you working with gardening? Understanding soil pH, texture, etc., may seem too much for
laymen, but it is essential for soil testing. This doesn't mean
you must be a scientist; simple DIY methods and professional services exist. Test for the soil pH using soil pH testing kits. Garden centres have these kits readily available and
are simple to use. Measuring soil acidity or alkalinity lets
you know whether you need to bring the soil into an optimal environment for your plants.

The other crucial step is to identify the soil texture.
Then, your soil will fall into three parts: clay, sandy, or
loamy. The particles in clay soils are microscopic, making
clay dense and nutrient-rich but unable to discharge water.

Drain well but not as wealthy in nutrients and usually have to be watered frequently; sandy soils contain larger particles. The two are balanced by loamy soil, the gardener's gold, which has good aeration, drainage, and nutrient retention. For instance, you can do a simple "jar test" at home to determine soil texture. Put soil and water in a clear jar, shake it, and let it settle. This will allow you to observe how the layers formed and the proportion of sand, silt, and clay.

To understand what your soil needs, it is important to analyze your soil nutrient levels, specifically the levels of nitrogen (N), phosphorus (P), and potassium (K). These nutrients are necessary for plants' growth, root development, and health. A DIY soil testing kit can provide you with a general sense, and depending on your needs, you might want to send a soil sample to a professional service for a more accurate and detailed analysis. Many soil tests are performed free or at a low cost, as most local county extension offices offer them. They provide detailed reports that will assist you in amending your soil.

One can enhance the soil if one understands its pH, texture, and nutrients. Materials added to soil for improved single properties are known as soil amendments. Com-post is perhaps the most widely known and beneficial of all the amendments. Organic matter is added, the structure of the soil is improved, and nutrients are provided. Lime can help bring the pH into a more suitable range for plants, thereby increasing the availability of nutrients allied to acidic soils. However, sulfur can reduce the pH of such alkaline soils. Clover or vetch are grown as green manure crops to goad the soil, then tilled to add organic matter and nutrients. Aeration and drainage are very important to root health, and materials such as vermiculite and perlite will increase aeration and drainage.

Plant growth depends highly on the structure of your soil. Either well-drained, aerated soil or container. Organic practices such as adding compost to improve soil structure and tending the soil by turning in organic matter will build a crumbly structure, hold moisture, and drain excess water. It is also important to avoid soil compaction. Compacting the soil inhibits root growth and inhibits water infiltration. Prevention is possible through simple techniques such as raising beds or incorporating organic matter.

It takes continuous effort to have healthy soil. To this extent, the soil remains fertile and well-structured by adding organic matter such as compost or well-rotting manure. Another effective practice is crop rotation. Rotating different types of crops every season prevents nutrient depletion in the soil keeps pests and diseases at bay, and allows you to use weaker alkalis instead of palm oil-based ones. Mulching is a very simple yet very powerful tool for soil health. Mulch makes a layer of mulch that helps retain moisture and suppresses weeds, and when it breaks down, the organic matter is added to the soil. Lastly, avoid over-tilling your soil. Occasional tilling can provide some benefits of incorporating organic matter, but excessive tilling can break up soil structure and the beneficial organisms.

Interactive Element: Soil Health Checklist

- **Soil pH Testing:** A soil pH testing kit checks if your soil is acidic, neutral, or alkaline.
- **Soil Texture Test:** The jar test determines the sand, silt, and clay measures in your soil.
- **Nutrient Analysis:** Getting detailed information about NPK levels would require the consideration of a professional soil test.

- **Compost Addition:** Build compost, and add compost to your soil as it gets added.
- **Crop Rotation Plan:** The first step you can take to increase the amount of soil you have is to come up with a crop rotation plan.
- **Mulching:** Mulching also helps to apply mulch to retain moisture and add organic matter.
- **Avoid Over-Tilling:** Till only as little as you need to till.

If you follow these guidelines, you will have a good and fertile place for your plants to have a productive and productive garden.

2.2 Composting 101: Turning Waste into Black Gold

Composting is a natural process in which organic waste is transformed into a rich soil conditioner called compost. Not only does this entire process reduce the amount of garbage you send off to the bottomless pit, but it also helps make your soil more insalubrious for your plants, making your plants more productive and healthier. Compost is black gold, a rich nutrient that can even turn the worst soil type into a garden bed that can grow a lush crop. Composting does not require chemical fertilizers and can reduce your need for them, which are harmful to the environment and your health. Instead, you build a natural, sustainable cycle of growth, harvest, and return to the earth of all nutrients.

Composting in your backyard is set up more than you may think, and several options suit your space and needs. The compost bins available in most homes are a great place to start. They are bins for you to hold and contain your composting material, and they may be made of wood, recycled plastic, or metal. They can be simple or elaborate, but good airflow will facilitate decomposition.

Tumbling composters are a good way for those who do not have the space or wish to be hands-on. Both can be turned to mix the composting materials and decelerate the decomposition process. Though there are many types of composters, those that require tumbling are particularly useful in an urban setting where space is premium and odours must be kept to a minimum.

If you are considering getting rid of your rubbish in an ecologically friendly way and using a very efficient process that will produce excellent high-quality compost, look no further than vermicomposting or worm composting. Vermicomposting is a method of breaking down organic waste using worms, mostly red .However, worm bins can be kept indoors or outdoors and are also ideal for snug spaces. They consume the waste and produce castings, which are highly nutritious compost.

If you're looking for an advanced composting method, then bokashi composting is worth inquiring about. This process involves using a mixture of microorganisms that turn organic waste, such as meat and dairy, which are not typically advised for conventional composting. Since they are compact and can be kept indoors, bokashi bins are perfect for apartment dwellers or people without outdoor space.

To succeed in utilizing the composting process, one must understand it. To compost the ingredients for good compost, you either need to balance browns (carbon-rich materials) and greens (nitrogen-rich materials), or you need not. Dried leaves, straw, and cardboard are browsers, kitchen scraps, grass clippings, and green coffee grounds. Essential is the proper layering of these materials. Browns first, then greens, etc... The ability to layer the compost pile correctly, with the right carbon-to-nitrogen ratio, is what this layering accomplishes the most.

It is also important that moisture levels are kept right. It should be as moist as a wrung-out sponge. Anaerobic decomposition with unpleasant odours can result from too much moisture, and the decomposition rate is decreased by too little humidity. Compost turns and aerates regularly to encourage the aerobic bacteria that will break down the organic matter; use a pitchfork or a compost turning tool to turn and mix materials well.

Making common composting troubleshooting saves a lot of your frustration. A bad-smelling compost pile is usually a result of a brown-to-green imbalance or a wet pile. But this problem can be solved by adding more browns and turning the pile. Securing your compost bin with a lid and burying food scraps in the pile's centre will deter pests like rodents and insects. Insufficient moisture or air can also result in slow decomposition, which can be accelerated simply by adjusting those factors. Finally, it is necessary to know when your compost is ready. Dark, crumbly, and earthy, finished compost should smell earthy. Garden beds can be enriched with top-dress lawns or included in potting mixes.

Case Study: Sarah's Urban Composting Success

Sarah, an urban dweller with very little outdoor space, decided to try vermicomposting. Red wigglers broke down her kitchen scraps within a worm bin, her initial worm bin. Less than a few months later, she had powerful, rich, perfect worm castings for her container garden. Her plants thrived, and she discovered that her waste output was much lower. Sarah's experience is that composting works in urban environments and can be rewarding.

So when you practice turning your organic waste into compost, you contribute to a higher degree of a sustainable lifestyle and a healthier garden. Composting is a waste reducer, and a recycle of growth and renewal, making your backyard homestead more productive and environmentally friendly. With a little time and the correct methods, you could convert waste into respectable, dark, great, and support sound, solid plant development.

∽◦

CHAPTER 3 RAISED BEDS AND CONTAINER GARDENING

One spring morning, I was standing in a corner of my yard holding a shovel and a stack of wooden planks in the other. This was my first adventure with raised beds since the solution changed my garden life. One of the benefits of having raised garden beds is poor soil conditions or limited space. It enables you to control supplementary soil quality, improve drainage, and reduce the strain of kneeling over to retrieve herbs. They can also be attractive, making an average yard a gorgeous, classy garden site.

3.1 Building and Maintaining Raised Garden Beds

When choosing what materials to use for your raised beds, there are a few to choose from, and they all have pros and cons. The two most popular are the topic of much debate: treated vs. untreated wood. Durability comes at a cost, with chemically treated timber, often still containing the chemicals designed to rot it or keep insects away, leaking chemicals into the soil. Many gardeners prefer untreated wood options such as cedar or redwood for peace of mind.

They are naturally rot-resistant and will last for years without chemical treatments. Another option, and still cheaper than picking new timber, is to leave your pine untreated, which will last a little while but needs replacing every couple of years.

Old crates and pallets, for example, can be recycled materials and cost-effective. They give a rustic feeling to your garden and contribute to reducing waste. There is, however, a caveat, as it's important that the wood hasn't been treated with harmful chemicals, especially if you are growing edible plants. If opting for stone or brick, they are durable and attractive. Although expensive and laborious to construct, they are very long, enduring, and stable. Another durable option is metal raised beds, which are usually constructed from galvanized steel. Pests are rot-resistant and tolerate hot conditions in direct sunlight, which is not ideal for all plants.

Building a raised bed should be easy enough with the right tools and a sense of patience. The first thing to do with the frame is cut and assemble the wooden planks. To do so, you'll need a saw, measuring tape, drill, and deck screws. Start by cutting the wood to lengths of your choosing. Its standard size is 4 times 8 feet and a height of about 12 to 18 inches. It is not too small or big and offers enough space for the roots to grow. Attach the side boards to the corner pieces with brackets to assemble the shorter ends. Next, combine the frames of the longer boards and shorter ends.

After it goes together, line the bottom with hardware cloth to deter gophers and moles from burrowing. Staple or nail the hardware cloth into place and overlap it to cover the entire bottom of the bed. The next is to fill the bed with a soil mix that allows good plant growth. Good mixing is done with garden soil, compost, and vermiculite. Structure, nutrients, aeration, and drainage are the three things garden soil provides; compost supplies nutrients, and vermiculite improves aeration and drainage. Peat moss can add more moisture retention, especially in drier climates.

Raised beds must be well drained to prevent waterlogging and resulting root rot. Make sure that the soil mix you use allows fluids to drain freely. Vermiculite and peat moss come into play here as they provide the balance of materials for the roots of the plants. Add compost or organic matter to your raised beds to maintain fertile, nutritious soil. Compost top dress the beds at the beginning of each growing season. Mix into the top a few inches of soil.

There are other effective methods to conserve moisture and prevent the growth of weeds, such as mulching. If you have no mulch layer around your plants, apply one—it will help lessen the impact of the hail. It helps to keep the soil moist, saves time watering, and displaces weeds. Maintaining soil health and not allowing pests and diseases to build up in the soil requires seasonal crop rotation. Plant different family vegetables in each bed area yearly, then rotate the crops. This practice facilitates nutrient use, balances nutrient use, and breaks pest and disease cycles.

Interactive Element: Raised Bed Maintenance Checklist

- **Add Compost Regularly:** Top-dress with compost at the start of each season.
- **Mulch Beds:** Apply organic mulch to conserve moisture and suppress weeds.
- **Rotate Crops Annually:** Change planting locations to maintain soil health.
- **Monitor for Pests:** Inspect plants regularly and take action at the first sign of trouble.

- **Weed Management:** Remove weeds promptly to reduce competition for nutrients.

Since raised beds are easier to control than traditional garden beds, their pest and weed management strategies are also easier. Its height helps some pests reach your plants, but the defined borders help eliminate weeds. However, vigilance is still necessary. Frequently visit your plants and eliminate pests as soon as you identify them. For where the pests are larger, hand pick or use organic pest control methods, like neem oil or insecticidal soap, for the smaller minor infestations.

Raised garden beds can transform your gardening experience in your building and during maintenance. Growing in raised beds is a great way to ensure that your crops will be lifted out of the mire, and there is little excuse not to reap the benefits of the raised beds for many years.

3.2 Container Gardening: Maximizing Small Spaces

Container gardening becomes a versatile and practical solution when space is at a premium. The first step is to choose the right containers. Many gardeners favour pots and planters. Different sizes, materials, or shapes are given to them. The various types of pot have their benefits. Terracotta pots are breathable but will dry out quickly. Lightweight and plastic pots keep moisture more than clay pots, making them easy to move around.

Other fantastic options include growing bags. They are breathable fabrics that allow excellent air circulation and stimulate healthy root systems. They are also easy to store when not in use. Trailing plants love hanging baskets as they save ground space. They can be hung from porch ceilings, balcony railings, and specially designated stands. Window boxes are functional and give a house curb appeal. They are perfect for herbs and small flowers, so plucking fresh ingredients right from your kitchen window is easy.

Including plants that need to be selected for your containers in your garden is vital. Container gardening also suits herbs like basil, mint, and rosemary. Placing them close to your kitchen will let you easily add fresh flavour to your meals, and they don't need much space. Cherry tomatoes and radishes are also suitable for container planting as they're small. In particular, cherry tomatoes do well in pots placed in the sun. Deep containers are also ideal for growing root crops like carrots and potatoes. If you're not into repositioning containers, consider using a grow bag for potatoes to make the potatoes as easy to harvest as dumping the bag.

Flowe and succulent plants in the container garden make your container garden beautiful. Petunias, geraniums, and marigolds will add brightness to any place, while succulents will be a great option for low-maintenance gardening. Moreover, they grow without much watering and can be grown in various container types, from small pots to large layouts.

Some specific techniques should be practised while planting and caring for container gardens. Begin with a top-quality container potting mix. Garden loam-packed and impeded root growth should be avoided. As containers do not discharge water down a drainage hole, the bottom must be covered in gravel or broken pottery for adequate drainage. One of the advantages is that it helps prevent water from pooling at the bottom, resulting in root rot.

Container gardens are difficult to water. Due to containers drying out faster than garden beds, watering must be done regularly. The size of your containers and also the size that your plants require will enable you to pay attention.

Daily watering may be required for smaller pots, while the larger ones may last a little longer. Stiff your finger into the soil about an inch and check the soil moisture regularly. Hollowed-out and dry are the signs of water. Another part of container gardening is fertilizing. Plants in containers can expel the nutrients in the soil quickly. Add balanced, water-soluble fertilizer every few weeks to keep your plants healthy and productive.

Container gardening is even more effective using creative solutions. The vertical space can be maximized with vertical planters - used materials like old wooden pallets or shoe organizers can be used to hang on walls or fences to become a green wall. Another innovative idea would be to DIY self-watering containers. They can be made by adding a water reservoir at the bottom of the container for plants to wick up to water as needed. This is extremely convenient for busy gardeners who forget to water frequently.

Compact hydroponic systems are ideal for those interested in soil-less gardening. These systems can be set up indoors or outdoors using nutrient-rich water, and plants can be grown. Growing leafy greens and herbs is what they are good at. The diverse combination of containers will add functionality and aesthetic upgrades to the garden. A bunch of different sizes and shapes of group pots together to make an attractive and productive group. Flowers can be grown with vegetables and herbs, look good, and promote a healthy garden ecosystem by attracting pollinators and beneficial insects.

Container gardening gives one opportunity for even the smallest space. Certain containers will offer lush and productive space for your garden, regardless of your space or lifestyle constraints, and some plants fit the space. Then, clever planting and care practices will be used to get the most creative from your space and lifestyle choices.

Container gardening allows you the flexibility and beauty. With this growth, any plant can be grown in less space, and it is a wonderful option for those in urban areas and people with a small yard since it provides more space. The care of herbs, vegetables, and flowers can be creative, and you can enjoy fresh herbs, vegetables, and flowers at your doorstep.

CHAPTER 4 VERTICAL GAR-DENING TECHNIQUES

Once, Mrs. Thompson visited my garden when it was spring and told me that it seemed to have sprouted up-wards, as she was saying, rather than outwards. She was curious, watching me turn my limited space into a lush vertical garden. I realized the impact of vertical gardening, especially when dealing with small areas, as she fascinated me. Vertical gardening has the magic of space efficiency, optimizing space and improving plants' health and aesthetic appearance in one pot.

4.1 Trellises and Arbors: Growing Up, Not Out

Trellises and arbours are both vertical structures that can make a difference in your gardening real estate regardless of the amount of space you have. Additionally, these structures help you plant multiple plants without extra square footage. The most significant advantage of this is it improves air circulation. Plants that grow upwards will have more access to fresh air, reducing their risk of fungal diseases. Healthier plants and fewer problems can be solved by better air circulation. Vertical gardening makes harvesting quite easy. If plants are grown on trellises, their fruits are hung down where one can easily pick them. Coming across ripe produce doesn't require bending over or digging through dense foliage. People with back problems or limited mobility appreciate that it is especially beneficial. This also decreases the risk of soil-borne diseases. The plants are off the ground, and thus, they will be less likely to touch contaminated soil. It keeps them healthier while reducing the need for chemical treatment.

Aside from that, they are aesthetically pleasing. Planting the same leading vegetables in a trellis covered with flowering vines or climbing vegetables will make a living wall both a garden and a piece of art. Additionally, they can offer privacy as natural screening between you and your neighbours. Think of yourself sitting in your backyard, walls all around you of greenery while having a cup of coffee. It is a nice, silent, beautiful way to kick-start the day.

You have many choices regarding materials and designs for arbours and trellises. One common wood to choose from is wood because it looks natural and is versatile. Since cedar and redwood are naturally rot-resistant, cedar and redwood are excellent options. Wrought iron or steel metal trellises provide durability and a classic look. Bamboo is a sustainable, cost-effective alternative to wooden structures that give your garden an exotic touch, even if you can mix materials to obtain a different design.

A personal garden can be achieved through DIY trellis designs. Wood or bamboo A-frame trellises are very simple to build and are ideal for growing peas or beans. A garden path has a more elaborate design, but you can use an arched trellis that spans the garden to improve it. Not only are you supporting your plants, but you will also create a beautiful focal point. Garden Centers and Online will offer premade options. Many come in different styles and sizes that you can pick from to match your needs and would also suit your taste. Your garden's modern rustic or traditional design can be customized to suit.

Success when choosing plants for the trellis and arbour depends on making the right choices. Vertical structures are the climbing vegetables — cucumbers, beans, and peas. Growing them forms them naturally into these candidates for trellises. Flowering vines like clematis and morning glory bring colour and fragrance to the garden. Once planted, these plants will quickly cover your trellis in brilliant blooms. Vertical growing of fruit-bearing plants like grapes and passion fruit is also possible. They look beautiful, and they are a delicious harvest. Perennial or annual climbers? It is to think of. Perennials such as climbing hydrangea and wisteria return year after year; annuals need to be planted annually but grow faster and are in bloom.

A bit of practical know-how involves installing and maintaining trellises and arbours. Especially with taller structures, stability is all that does. If needed, use concrete to make your posts for your trellis or arbour so that they are sunk very deep into the ground. Then, secure your trellis or arbour to your anchor posts. To further stabilize, ground spikes or guy wires may be used. It is a simple but essential task to train plants to climb. Tie the stems to the trellis with soft ties or garden twine, gently tracing the direction you desire the stems to grow. When growing plants, keep on tying up new growth on the structure.

Drawing plants makes them healthier and easier to maintain a shaped look. Discard dead or sick branches to stimulate healthy advancement. After flowering vines, pruning will tidy them up and encourage more flowers next season. Some seasonal maintenance tasks are checking for any damage to the trellis or arbour and making the necessary repairs. These structures need to be inspected in early spring to determine if they are doomed and are reinforced with lag screws if necessary.

Interactive Element: Vertical Gardening Checklist

- **Assess Space:** Identify areas in your garden where vertical structures can be added.
- **Select Materials:** Choose wood, metal, or bamboo based on your garden's style.
- **Build or Buy:** Decide whether to DIY or purchase pre-made trellises or arbours.
- **Choose Plants:** Select climbing vegetables, flowering vines, or fruit-bearing plants.
- **Install Securely:** Anchor your trellis or arbour firmly to withstand wind and growth.
- **Train Plants:** Use soft ties to guide plants as they grow.
- **Prune Regularly:** Keep plants healthy and promote growth by regular pruning.
- **Seasonal Maintenance:** Check and repair structures annually, especially after winter.

You can transform even the smallest spaces into lush, productive, and beautiful areas by incorporating trellises and arbours into your garden. Vertical gardening not only maximizes your growing area but also enhances the health and accessibility of your plants.

4.2 Wall Gardens and Green Towers

Imagine that your backyard wall is blank, and you stand one looking. However, proper techniques can make that unused vertical space a lush, green garden. Wall gardens and green towers are perfect for those with limited ground space but still want to grow more as these apply to individuals with limited space. They permit you to garden upwards, transforming walls and vertical spaces into productive, beautiful green spaces. Moreover, they save space and provide urban gardening solutions for different plants, even in a city setting. Secondly, a walled garden or a green tower provides decorative and functional benefits. It adds a spectacular visual display, improving the surrounding area around your home and the microclimate.

Different wall gardens and green towers are found, some having different characteristics and benefits. Popular are living walls, also referred to as green or modular systems. Another form of these structures falls into 'panels or modules that can be mounted to walls and filled with soil and planted with vegetation.' Living walls can be designed with any shape and crafted to fit your space so that they can be fitted into either a small balcony or a large outdoor one. Natural air purifiers help to improve air quality and absorb sound waves, and they also work to reduce noise pollution. However, they are quite fussy and must be carefully planned and maintained to become frosted.

Using the benefits of pocket planters for vertical gardening is also a good idea. Wall buckets or great walls can be tied to a fence or wall filled with soil and plants. It is great for herbs, small veggies, and flowers. Pocket planters are easier to install and maintain, making them a good beginner's option. Additionally, they are extremely cheap and can be made of recycled items like old shoe organizers or fabric pockets, making your garden a little more eco-friendly.

Vertical gardening with plant growing using nutrient water is rich in hydroponic wall gardens. These systems are particularly suitable for growing leafy greens and herbs as they are clean and efficient growing plant systems. Indoor and poor soil quality setups are perfect for using hydroponic wall gardens. However, the method does come associated with an initial investment: equipment such as water pumps and nutrient solutions — but at the cost of faster plant growth and higher yields. This is particularly good when they avoid the risk of soil-born diseases or pests, as hydroponic systems are a low-maintenance option.

Vertical gardening structures such as stackable green towers increase the number of plants that can be grown in space by effectively stacking several layers of plants. These towers normally come in plastic or metal and can be stacked to the desired height. It is a compact space separated between layers, and you can garden in each space with different plants. They are great for strawberries, herbs, and smaller vegetables growing in stackable green towers. Most come with pre-built irrigation systems, so your plants are getting good moisture and are easy to assemble. These towers are designed so modularly that they can be placed in various spaces, from small patios to veritable gardens.

To be a success in wall gardens and green towers, plants must be chosen correctly. These setups are a great fit for herbs and leafy greens because they grow quickly and have shallow root systems. Pocket planters and hydroponic walls are just what basil, mint, parsley, and lettuce are all great at. Confined spreading space brings up their perfect habitat as they can be harvested regularly for fresh, homegrown flavour. Also suitable for vertical gardening are drought-tolerant plants, including succulents and certain flowers. This lanky group of plants is low maintenance and resilient, takes less water, and can withstand the challenge of being grown in a vertical setup.

One way of adding some visual appeal to your wall garden is to add flowering plants. Nasturtium, petunia, and marigold are plants that can add some colours. There are a couple of ways to use watering and fertilizing techniques, which are very important for care. Due to drier vertical gardens, this type of garden requires more regular watering than a ground garden. A drip irrigation system allows you to install and ensure your plant receives constant water. Fertilizing is also needed, especially for hydroponic systems. But giving your child one that's imbalanced, water-insoluble, and can lead to harm is not recommended.

A rewarding DIY project is creating a walled garden or a green tower. Choose a suitable place with enough sunshine and water nearby. You can use wooden pallets or old gutters to use recycled materials for a DIY wall garden. These materials will attach to your wall; you will put soil and plants in them. Drill holes at the bottom of each container for proper drainage. You should consider purchasing commercial wall garden systems for a more compact look. These come in different designs and sizes and can be easily installed. These popular examples include Woolly Pocket's modular systems and FloraFelt's vertical garden planters, which people love because they are easy to use and durable.

Additional considerations exist for installing a wall garden or green tower indoors. Check that the wall can withstand the weight of the garden when it is filled with soil and water. Waterproof liners/trays are used so that water does not damage walls and floors. Place the garden close to a window with a lot of light or a grow light to ensure enough light for your plants. It's important to regularly examine for signs of mould or mildew as indoor setups are susceptible to high humidity.

Vertical gardening in its truest will see you getting wall gardens and green towers that blend high functionality with beauty. They do so by turning a good, if limited, space into urban gardening solutions and making the most stunning visual displays out of accessible areas. With the right plant selection and proper care, you can enjoy a lush, productive garden that complements your living space.

Wall gardening and green towers go a long way to increasing vertical gardening in your home while bringing nature to the urban areas. The next chapter will discuss efficient water management techniques to make your backyard farming experience more enjoyable.

CHAPTER 5 EFFICIENT WATER MANAGEMENT

The summer that the sun was, I decided to turn everything in my garden to crisp. My water bill went up, yet here I was, struggling to keep many plants from wilting in the midday sun. At that moment, I found it out: drip irrigation — a holy grail for a serious gardener who needs to save water. In this chapter, we take you through the process of doing it yourself with a DIY drip irrigation system and show you how to water your plants using less time, money, and resources.

5.1 DIY Drip Irrigation Systems

Drip irrigation is a system of watering that disperses water in one drop, drip at a time, to the roots of your plants. This ultimate garden utilitarian tool has several advantages that make it extremely useful for gardeners, particularly those with scarce access to water or a small garden area to work within. The main advantage is water efficiency. Drip systems differ from traditional sprinklers that can waste water from evaporation and runoff, and water can be applied where needed. Targeting your water waste minimizes your water waste to every drop.

Furthermore, drip irrigation also prevents soil erosion. By delivering water slowly and directly into the soil, you minimize the risks of surface runoff that can knock it away, as well as topsoil and nutrients. Another key benefit of this caddie is that it will always have consistent moisture levels. A drip system ensures that plants have a steady water supply, ensuring their survival. It ensures healthy plant growth, resulting in more abundant harvests. Drip irrigation also keeps the foliage dry and away from fungal diseases, which prefer humid surroundings. The fewer pests, the healthier the plants will be on the whole.

Because it seems so complex to set up a DIY drip irrigation system, I thought I should put this post together to help answer some beginner questions and define some of the parts you will need. The backbone of the system consists of the mainline tubing. That flexible pipe reaches different parts of your garden and distributes water from the source. The tubing is made into dippers and emitters, which control water flow to the plants. Drippers only drip slowly and steadily; emitters can be set differently to give different amounts depending on the plant's needs. It serves as a connector between different system tubes to be safe and leakproof. A pressure regulator is needed to maintain the same water pressure so that you do not get blowouts or water that is not distributed evenly. The last thing is that a timer automates the watering schedule and eliminates the guesswork around how much and when to water your garden.

Planning the layout is the first method to build your drip irrigation system. It will also depend on your plants' spacing and water needs. Water plants of similar water requirements together. Once you have a plan, make your way with stakes to secure the mainline tubing along the garden beds. If necessary, the tubing can be severed to the desired length and subsequently joined via connectors. Then, quickly work through the tubing, making punch holes where you want to direct drippers or emitters. Put the drippers or emitters into the holes, and they are securely attached.

Though it might seem hard to get a drip irrigation system done, it is not a big deal if you know how to work on the components. The backbone of the system consists of the mainline tubing. That flexible pipe reaches different parts of your garden and distributes water from the source. The tubing is made into dippers and emitters, which control water flow to the plants. Drippers only drip slowly and steadily; emitters can be set differently to give different amounts depending on the plant's needs. It serves as a connector between different system tubes to be safe and leakproof. A pressure regulator is needed to maintain the same water pressure so that you do not get blowouts or water that is not distributed evenly. An additional step finally takes the guesswork out of when and for how long you water your garden by automating the watering schedule using a timer.

Planning the layout is the first method to build your drip irrigation system. Think about the spacing and what your plants require in terms of water. Water plants of similar water requirements together. Once you have a plan, make your way with stakes to secure the mainline tubing along the garden beds. If necessary, the tubing can be severed to the desired length and subsequently joined via connectors. Then, quickly work through the tubing, making punch holes where you want to direct drippers or emitters. Put the drippers or emitters into the holes, and they are securely attached.

Interactive Element: Drip Irrigation Maintenance Checklist

- **Check for Clogs:** Inspect drippers and emitters weekly.
- **Flush the System:** Remove the end cap and flush out debris monthly.
- **Inspect Connections:** Tighten any loose fittings and check for leaks.
- **Adjust Drippers:** Move drippers closer to the root zone as plants grow.
- **Test the Timer:** Ensure the timer is working correctly and set to the proper schedule.

Implementing a DIY drip irrigation system allows you to water your garden more efficiently, reduce water waste, and promote healthier plant growth. This system is particularly beneficial for those with limited space or water resources, making it a valuable tool for any backyard farmer.

5.2 Rainwater Harvesting and Greywater Recycling

The day I watched rain pour off my roof and flood the yard into a puddle, I suddenly realized there would be a lot of wasted water. That realization drove my exploration into rainwater harvesting, a simple idea that has a huge impact on using the greatest gift of nature. It is an easy idea: accumulate, store, and use rainwater when required. This method drastically reduces your dependence on municipal water supplies during a drought or water restrictions. On top of that, it also helps bring down your water bills, thus making your homestead more self-sufficient. In addition, collecting rainwater lowers the amount of stormwater runoff that can cause erosion and transport pollutants into the waterways.

Even for small spaces, rainwater harvesting is easier than you imagine and fairly straightforward to set up. First, select suitable rain barrels or tanks. Garden centres or online, these sizes vary from 50 to 90 gallons. Place barrels under downspouts to capture as much water as possible. Fitted with sturdy stands and elevated, the barrels may assist with water flow by the momentum of gravity, which makes for easier water access.

Then, gutter diverters are installed to send the rainwater toward the storage barrels. These devices are easily strapped to your existing gutters and direct water into your barrels while filtering out big debris. In addition, fine mesh filters should be added at the entry points to prevent smaller debris from getting in. These filters filter out the leaves, twigs, and insects from your water supply. Heavy rains need to be dealt with by overflow outlets. These outlets would be installed to send the surplus water to your home's foundation to avoid potential damage.

Harvested rainwater effectively can impact the job in your backyard homestead in a very significant way. The most common usage is watering your garden and lawn. Rainwater is naturally soft and contains no chemical chlorides or fluoride, making it ideal for plants. It also provides a great way to fill your ponds or water features, bringing an attractive, eco-friendly landscape. Rinsing the outdoor areas and tools with rainwater decreases your dependence on tap water and keeps your tools clean. Automating your watering process becomes possible by connecting rain barrels to a drip irrigation system so your plants can retain moisture without any extra effort.

Greywater recycling is another innovative way of conserving water. Slightly used water from sinks, showers, and laundry, excluding toilet waste, is known as grey water. Using grey water to water your garden saves on freshwater and decreases the volume of wastewater discharged into the sewer or septic system. It's a good practice for a sustainable lifestyle and can help save your water bills tremendously.

Globally, greywater recycling has its own set of challenges and considerations. The first step is to find suitable sources of greywater in your home. Showers, bathtubs, and washing machines are generally good water for irrigation as long as it doesn't have harsh chemicals. It must also be run through a filtering device to some extent, which can be Dishwater, though it may need a bit more filtration to get out the food particles and grease. Never put water with bleach, borax, or high sodium in them, as it may damage your soil and plants.

The legal and local regulations are very important when installing a greywater system. Greywater use has specific guidelines or requires permits in some of the regions. Also, confirm if your area is compliant and avoid legal issues, then check with your local authorities. They are also paramount with regard to health and safety precautions. Bacterial growth should be avoided, and greywater should be used within 24 hours. It's never to be sprayed onto edible parts of plants and is best applied directly to the soil. Do not use greywater on root crops or young, delicate plants that may be sensitive to contaminants.

Greywater can be made safer for its use with basic treatment methods. Using a simple settling tank, solids will settle out at the bottom, and you won't clog your irrigation system with solids. You can further clean the water with a filter, such as a cloth bag or a commercial water filter. Chlorine or iodine are disinfectants, but they should be used carefully to avoid damaging plants. Maintaining a greywater system by regularly cleaning or replacing the filters is important.

Integrating rainwater harvesting and greywater recycling nourishes your backyard homestead with life, and you are on your way to a sustainable life. Moreover, these methods save your precious water and increase the homestead´s resiliency and self-sufficiency. Whether harvesting rainwater from your garden to water it or using greywater to irrigate, these works contribute to efficiently using your available water, less waste, and a healthier environment.

CHAPTER 6 SEASONAL PLANT-
ING AND CROP ROTATION

One spring evening, I stood in front of a seed display at the local garden centre, overwhelmed by the sheer variety of options. A seasoned gardener was nearby and offered me some wisdom that changed my approach to gardening: "The key to a thriving garden is planting at the right time." Understanding the growing seasons and how they affect planting schedules is crucial for maximizing your garden's productivity, especially when working with limited space.

6.1 Seasonal Planting Guides

Being able to grow seasonally is very important in gardening. Each season incites a challenge and an opportunity. The growing seasons are mainly controlled by temperature and daylight hours. Temperatures slowly warm, making it warmer and warmer as it goes, and it gets lighter and lighter, almost building to the point of being able to plant cold season crops. Heat and prolonged days are ideal for growing warm vegetables and fruits in the summer. The super cool fall is also marked by cooler temperatures and shorter days, which are good for hardy crops. In winter, the garden can be a rest period where it's cold and there is little daylight. But it can also be a time to start plants grown from seed that will be protected and develop cold, hardy vegetables.

It is, therefore, important to know your area's frost dates to plan your planting schedule. The origins of the average frost dates are from sources like the Old Farmer's Almanac on historical climate data. Having these dates at hand lets you understand when to start growing and when the growing season will end. For example, in areas with a date for the last spring frost well into late April, you can grow cool-season crops as early as the last week in March. On the other hand, if you knew the first fall frost date, you will not plant in the fall unless you want them to be mature before you have a cold.

Plants are planted at different times depending on different climates. In warmer climates, some crops will grow year-round. However, cooler climates have shorter growing seasons, so every available time has to be planned as carefully as possible. Planting might also be affected by microclimates within your backyard. The new wall could also create a warmer microclimate that would enable you to plant some crops earlier or stay in the growing season later than other parts of your yard. You can pay attention to these microclimates to optimize your garden's productivity.

In spring, cool-season crops and early starters come alive in the garden. Early spring has mild temperatures for leafy greens such as spinach and lettuce. These greens can be sown directly once the garden soil can be worked. They are also suitable root crops, such as root vegetables like carrots and radishes. Carrots also appreciate early planting, given their long growing season, but radishes are a quick crop that rewards quickly. Early-season herbs, such as dill and parsley, can be sown in the garden or started indoors to give an early start to the season.

The technique of starting seeds indoors assists early spring planting. From late February through early March, one can start crops such as kale, broccoli, cauliflower, onions, fennel, and lettuce indoors. Use seed starting mix of fine texture in cell trays or flats. These seedlings are ready to be transplanted into the garden in mid-April after four to six weeks. This gives your plants a head start in that the root system is strong and able to withstand moving the plants outdoors.

During summer, we start to think of warm-season vegetables and fruits. Summer staples in any garden are tomatoes and peppers that can withstand heat. Mid to late March, this can be started indoors and transplanted outdoors after the danger of frost. Besides cucumbers and squash, other good things to plant in the summer are members of the gourd family. Direct seeds of these vegetables may be dropped into the garden or started indoors to get an earlier, higher harvest. Traditionally, beans and corn become summer crops that appreciate the long, hot days. Corn is a little more space hog, but you get sweet, delicious ears for your efforts, and beans can be planted directly into the soil.

Succession planting maintains a constant harvest throughout the summer. This allows you to have fresh produce all season if you plant small batches of crops like beans, cucumbers, and lettuce every two to three weeks. In addition, this method also helps to manage the workload so that you are not overwhelmed by one big harvest.

With fall approaching and summer waning, it's about time to contemplate the possibilities to extend the growing season. Cold, hardy crops like broccoli and cabbage will grow in the fall. In mid-summer, indoors, these vegetables can be planted and transplanted into the garden sometime in late summer or early fall. Beets and turnips are also great fall-to-plant root vegetables. Direct sowing of beets into the garden or turnips take advantage of the cooler temperature.

To protect your growing fall and winter crops from frost, row covers and cold frames are a good bet. Frost protection can be afforded by row covers of lightweight fabrics draped over plants, which supply a few degrees of protection from frost. Cold frames are a mini greenhouse that traps heat and prolongs the growing season. Overwintering crops like spinach and kale are very beneficial because they allow you to harvest fresh greens in the depths of winter.

Overwintering crops is a way to ensure a spring win over early crops. Cold frames or heavy mulch will allow cold, hardy crops like spinach, kale, and carrots to survive over winter. By early spring, these crops will begin to grow again and be harvested early to allow farmers to reap an early harvest before the start of the new season's plantings.

By knowing your lying season, you can shift your proportions of planting. Knowing the temperature, daylight hours, and when to expect frost dates will allow you to do most of each season. Spring gardening requires cool-season greens, summer gardening requires warm-season vegetables, and fall and winter gardening requires hardy crops; in all cases, they require planning and timing to get productive and rewarding crops. Welcome the seasons of your life, and they will never not grow.

6.2 Crop Rotation for Soil Health

Sustainable gardening is based on crop rotation. So, changing the types of crops grown in the specific areas of your garden from year to year is called this practice. Rotating crops breaks pest and disease cycles, prevents soil nutrient depletion, improves soil structure, and helps increase the diversity of your garden. Different types of plants require different nutrients from the soil, and without rotation, the same plants continue to deplete the same nutrients, which leads to unhealthy soil in the end. Rotating crops changes the nutrients depleted from the soil, giving them a chance to rest and rebuild their vital nutrients.

Crop rotation also has the great advantage of breaking pest and disease cycles. Host-specific pests and diseases target only certain types of plants. With the same crop in the same spot over and over, weeds and diseases can build up in the soil and create huge infestations. Rotating crops and thus disrupting these cycles decreases the possibility of the occurrence of pests and diseases. For instance, skipping one location yearly will allow for soil-borne disease build-up, such as verticillium wilt with tomatoes. This issue can be mitigated by rotating the plant with a non-host crop such as beans.

Taking crop rotation into account, soil structure and organic matter also improve. Because different plants have different root structures and growth habits, different plants will aerate the soil and prevent compacting to differing degrees. Carrots, parsnips, and other deep-rooted plants break up the soil, and peas and beans, among the legumes, add nitrogen to the soil, making it richer for future crops. This diversity of plant species helps a more resilient soil ecosystem. Crop rotation increases the biodiversity in your garden, creating a healthy balance that allows beneficial organisms to thrive, increasing plant health and product.

Crop rotation takes some organization but offers healthier soil and plants. Grouping crops by family first will help start your рукописное задание: семинары ро d (PDF) assignment since plants in the same family tend to have similar nutrient requirements and pest problems. This is the case in the nightshade family, for tomatoes, peppers, eggplants, beans, and peas are part of the legume family. Rotating these families also means eliminating the draining of the same nutrients every year. Then, rotate heavy feeders, light feeders, and soil builders. Corn and tomatoes need a lot of nutrients, and I give them a lot of nutrients, and carrots and radishes need a very minimum of them, and I give them very little, so I feed heavy foods, thereby, heavy feeders. Legumes are soil builders that add nutrients back into it. By moving them around, they stay in balance regarding the nutrient profile in your soil.

A multi-year rotation plan also helps you with organization, and no crop family is planted and genetically in the same location for several years. Maybe something simple in light of four-year rotations: Year 1 would be Nightshades, Year 2 would be Legumes, Year 3 would be Brassicas, Year 4 Root Vegetables. Adjust the cycle by repeating it as needed for your garden needs. It is very important to keep a detailed record of the location of crops to manage rotation more effectively. Use a garden journal or digital tool so each crop is planted in the same place yearly. Bill Lowe heads up Clemson University in South Carolina, where they mainly plant in fields featuring doubled rows, although I have also seen instances of single rows.

Implementing cover crops is another powerful way to increase soil health and fertility. Typically, cover crops are grown to improve the soil and not to be harvested. Nutrient fixes, erosion control, weed suppression, and tolerance to chemical applications are some of their many benefits. For instance, legumes such as clover and vetch are added to the soil to fix nitrogen and enrich it for future crops. The soil from erosion is protected as fast-growing annual rye and radishes improve soil structure. You must choose cover crops based on that season and what you specifically need. You could plant winter rye in the fall to mulch the soil in winter and feed it in the spring. Buckwheat can be a quick-growing cover crop that also suppresses weeds in the summer.

Planting and terminating cover crops are done in a variety of ways. Alternatively, you can broadcast seeds over the soil and loosely rake in or use a seed drill for more accurate planting. When the cover crop has grown, terminating it by mowing, cutting, or tilling it into the soil will occur. The green manuring process adds organic matter and nutrients to the soil, which helps improve the fertility and structure of the soil. Residues from cover crops can be incorporated into the soil several weeks before growing your main crops so that the time spent decomposing the residue will give you more time after planting to be mindful of the soil needs of your crops.

While some dexterity is required to adapt crop rotation to small spaces, it's entirely doable. Rotation is flexible in raised beds and containers. Raised beds can quickly be moved into containers, or the soil can be changed to different crops yearly. Both intercropping and companion planting are excellent ways of maximizing space and improving the health of soils. Intercropping is to grow lettuce between the rows of tomatoes in the same space. Companion planting involves planting two or more plants together, as with basil and tomatoes, as both repel pests.

However, managing crop rotation in vertical gardens may be more difficult, but it is possible. Rotate crops within each vertical tier or section you have. For example, one year, if you are growing strawberries in a vertical tower, then install lettuce or herbs in that area of the tower the following year. Key to the adjustment of rotation plans based on garden size and layout. For smaller gardens, more frequent rotation or creative ways might be needed, such as covering crops in containers during off-seasons. No matter your space size, the goal is to keep the soil healthy and productive.

Crop rotation with the addition of cover crops can keep the soil healthy, reduce the pressure of pests and diseases, and make the garden more resilient. It is important to note that these practices are the most foundational thing towards being a sustainable gardener and also a great practice for folks who may not have a lot of space.

With these principles, thoughtfully planning your garden is the beginning of a thriving, sustainable homestead. We next explore plant nutrients and soil amendments, further breaching how to keep soil healthy and plants happy.

⤚∞

CHAPTER 7 PLANT NUTRIENTS AND SOIL AMENDMENTS

The first time I noticed my tomato plants turning yellow, I felt a wave of frustration wash over me. I had done everything right—or so I thought. It wasn't until I delved into the world of plant nutrients that I realized my garden's struggles weren't a lack of effort but a lack of understanding. Plants, much like us, need a balanced diet to thrive. This chapter will guide you through the essential nutrients your plants need and how to ensure they get them.

7.1 Essential Plant Nutrients and Their Sources

Nitrogen (N), phosphorus (P), and potassium (K) are the three main macronutrients that a plant needs to grow strong and healthy. Each one of these nutrients is important to the plant's development. Leafy green growth requires nitrogen. Nitrogen is the missing piece to lush lettuce or spinach if you have ever wondered why your lettuce or spinach isn't as lush as you would like. The chlorophyll plant uses this to convert sunlight into energy, a large component. You can also do so in the soil if you can provide nitrogen through organic processes such as compost or green manures like clover or alfalfa.

On this hand, phosphorus is needed for root development and flowering. It is essential at the tender early stages of plant growth when roots develop normally and at other stages when plants set flowers and fruit. Despite how healthy plants look, they might not transfer into a flowering or fruit-bearing stage. This phosphorus source can come from fancy bone meal, rock phosphate, bat guano, wood ash, or blood and bone meal. These amendments are vital to your plant's development, root system, flowering, and fruiting!

Potassium makes the plant healthier and increases disease resistance. It helps regulate certain physiological processes like water uptake, enzyme activation, and photosynthesis. Leaves with browning from the leaf edge may indicate that plants are easily infected with diseases if they are deficient in potassium. Organic sources of potassium include wood ash, greensand, and kelp meal. These can be incorporated into your soil for greater resistance and productivity.

Plants also require secondary macronutrients like calcium (Ca), magnesium (Mg), and sulfur (S) to survive, in addition to the primary macronutrients. Calcium helps fortify cell walls against blossom end rot, a disease that affects tomatoes and peppers. This is a nutrient essential for the structural integrity of plants so that the plant can support the leaves and fruit branches. Good sources of calcium include eggshells, gypsum, lime, etc. They can be added to your soil to prevent calcium deficiencies and help them grow strong.

Chlorophyll is essential for the production of chlorophyll to get plants photosynthesizing efficiently. Without enough magnesium, plants cannot produce the energy they need to grow. Magnesium, as well as the good, comes from Epsom salts and dolomitic lime. They can be easily dissolved in water for a foliar spray or dissolved in your soil.

Protein synthesis and enzyme function depend upon sulfur. Also, it is necessary to produce specific vitamins, which are raw materials for the biosynthesis of sex hormones and amino acids, in plants. Less common but possible, sulfur deficiencies occur in sandy soils or areas with high rainfall. This nutrient is derived from elemental sulfur or gypsum. These should be added to your soil to bring your plants the sulfur they require for healthy growth and development.

While micronutrients are necessary in lesser amounts, they are just as important for the health of the plants. Included in them are boron (B), copper (Cu), iron (Fe), manganese (Mn), molybdenum (Mo), and zinc (Zn). Boron helps in forming cell walls and reproductive development. Fruit and seed set is poor when there is a lack of boron. Good sources of boron are borax and compost. Generally, it was found that iron for chlorophyll synthesis is critical for plant green colour and energy production. Iron deficiencies are corrected with the common use of iron sulfate and chelated iron.

But closely watching your plants can explain 'nutrient deficiency.' Typically, leaves that turn yellow are a sign of nitrogen deficiency. If your plants lose their colour and appear stunted and pale, and their older leaves, in particular, look pale, consider adding a nitrogen-rich amendment. If flowering or fruiting is poor, phosphorus may be in short supply. Ensure your soil has enough organic phosphorus for the most critical stages. Potassium deficiency can be indicated by leaf edge browning. If you observe this symptom, make a point to add potassium-rich additions to your dirt. Causes of calcium or magnesium deficiency include stunted growth and distorted new leaves. Calcium or magnesium sources can be added to correct these problems and promote healthy growth.

Visual Element: Nutrient Deficiency Symptoms Chart

- **Nitrogen Deficiency:** Yellowing of older leaves, stunted growth
- **Phosphorus Deficiency:** Poor flowering, purplish leaves
- **Potassium Deficiency:** Browning of leaf edges, weak stems
- **Calcium Deficiency:** Blossom end rot, distorted new leaves
- **Magnesium Deficiency:** Yellowing between leaf veins, older leaves affected
- **Iron Deficiency:** Yellowing of new leaves, green veins

Addressing these deficiencies involves more than just adding fertilizers. It's about understanding your soil and creating a balanced environment where plants thrive. Regular soil testing can help you monitor nutrient levels and make informed decisions about amendments. You can ensure a healthy, productive garden by paying attention to the signs your plants give you and providing the nutrients they need.

7.2 DIY Soil Amendments and Fertilizers

Turning scraps into soil amendments can bring the bang of a dragger to your backyard homestead. Homemade is cheaper, but even more importantly, you have complete control of custom nutrient blends to suit your garden's needs. This is sustainable and eco-friendly because it often employs household and garden waste that would have otherwise ended up in landfills. You make your soil amendments and thus gain charge over what goes in your garden; charge that your plants get the best possible care and minimalize your environmental footprint.

A compost is perhaps one of the most effective ways of improving soil health and fertility. High-quality compost may be produced using advanced composting techniques that enrich soil with organic nature and essential nutrients. In hot composting, a compost pile is maintained at high temperatures so that the decomposition process takes place speedily. You must balance a green (nitrogen-rich) and brown (carbon-rich) mix to get this. Regularly turning the pile to make oxygen available to all the organic matter ensures that the activity of the organisms that break it down always works. Adding nutrient-rich compost to your garden beds can be done in a few weeks.

Another excellent way to produce nutrient-fulfillment compost is vermicomposting or worm composting. Using worms or red wigglers to 'break down' kitchen scraps and garden waste by this technique. The worms consume organic material, and castings are produced, which are nutrient-rich. Indoors or outdoors, these will be kept properly for gardeners with limited space. The worm castings can be mixed into the soil or brewed as a compost tea, a liquid-liquid fertilizer to promote plant growth.

Compost teas are a great addition to your plant-feeding routine. To create compost tea, steep the compost in water for a number of days, letting the microorganisms and nutrients leach into the liquid. This makes for a quick nutrient boost for your plants, either directly on the soil or as a foliar spray. It is very useful during the growing season when plants must be pushed to reach their fullest potential.

Composting kitchen scraps and garden waste into your routine will help reduce waste and enhance your compost with essential nutrition. Vegetable peelings, coffee grounds, egg shells, and grass clippings are good additions. Don't put meat, dairy, or rancid foods onto the pile because they attract insects and slow fermentation. You can add these materials to your compost pile or bin regularly, and your supply of nutrient-rich compost will continue.

Another effective way to be sure your plants get the required nutrients is to make homemade fertilizers for your garden. It is good to use Fish emulsion fertilizer as a common way to boost nitrogen. It is a liquid fertilizer made from fish waste and is high in nitrogen, encouraging leafy green growth. Blend fish scraps and water and leave it to ferment for several weeks to make a fish emulsion. Apply the liquid to your garden after strain and dilute.

Banana peel fertilizer is a good potassium boost. One essential plant nutrient found in banana peels is potassium. Banana peels are chopped and placed in water for a few days to make this fertilizer. Pour the liquid into a strainer and water your plants as an available potassium source.

Caused by insufficient calcium, blossom end rot causes the darkening at the end of your tomato's blossom and is perfectly prevented by calcium from an eggshell. To prepare an eggshell calcium amendment, rinse and dry eggshells and then grind the eggshells into a fine powder. Use powdered eggshells to help provide a slow-release source of calcium to your plants; sprinkle the powdered eggshells around them or work them into the soil.

Full natural fertility and structure can be given to the soil by green manures and cover crops. Plant legumes such as clover and vetch to fix nitrogen in the soil. The bacteria that these plants have symbiotic relationships with can fix nitrogen, which air plants cannot do. Cover crops based on legumes improve soil fertility without synthetic fertilizers.

Another good cover crop is buckwheat, which also helps suppress weeds and provides organic matter. The growth is fast, so the foliage is also dense enough that the weeds cannot have their chance. What this means is that there is less need to use herbicides. TF Green: when tilled into the soil, Buckwheat is broken down quickly to add a vast amount of organic material and enhance soil structure.

Mixing or tilling in cover crops (green manures) is a very important Gardening step. When the cover crop matures, cut it and incorporate it into the soil. With the addition of organic matter and nutrients, soil structure and fertility are improved. If you keep the timing right, you will have a few weeks for the cover crop to break down once the main crops are planted.

These DIY soil amendments and fertilizers can help make you a thriving, productive garden. However, the way to proper plant health is to take a hands-on approach to soil health, as you will ensure your plants get the necessary nutrients and help promote sustainability and waste reduction.

By understanding the intricate balance of nutrients and utilizing homemade solutions, you lay the foundation for a robust, thriving garden. Next, we'll delve into the practicalities of organic pest control, ensuring that your hard work doesn't go to waste.

CHAPTER 8 ORGANIC PEST CONTROL

Once, I witnessed a heap of aphids descending on my precious tomato plants that summer. It seemed like they were unstoppable, but as I went on with my best efforts to stop them, I knew it wouldn't be through harsh chemicals. That's when I learned about companion planting, the dry and effective way to lock away pests without relying on chemical pesticides and create a healthy garden society. Companion planting is placing selected plants in strategic pairs to help each other's growth, repel harmful insects, call for good insects, and improve soil health. This method encourages a balanced garden that is a bit more productive and resilient.

8.1 Companion Planting for Pest Control

Gardening is planting different species of plants close to each other to provide a conducive environment for them. The idea is for a healthier and more productive garden, allowing for plant growth aid, pest repelling, and attracting beneficial insects. Companion planting mimics the natural ecosystems, increases biodiversity, and minimizes the need for chemical interventions. This sustainable and eco-friendly approach can be applied to small home plots and larger homesteads.

Companion planting has one of the main benefits of improving plant growth and health. Some plants emit chemicals or scents that positively influence their neighbours to grow but to grow larger and yield more. For instance, marigold produces thiophene, which repels nematodes, aphids, and white flies. Suppose you want to protect tomatoes and peppers from these common pests; plant marigolds near susceptible crops. Another strong companion plant that repels mosquitoes and flies is basil. Basil planted near tomatoes is not only a pest deterrent but also enhances the flavour of the tomatoes.

Finally, companion planting attracts beneficial insects that suppress pest populations organically. An example is the nasturtiums, which are great at drawing aphids for all main crops at all times. In return for that, these flowers are trap crops - they lure aphids to them and away from your vegetables. Garlic and onions are also very strong, smelling and repel aphids and slugs. You can deter pest flies near vulnerable crops geothermally by planting aromatic alliums. Using a diversity of companion plants creates a diverse habitat where beneficial insects, such as ladybugs, lacewings, and parasitic wasps that eat common garden pests, can live.

Another great compliment to companion planting is that it improves your soil health by doing so. Nutrient-poor soil can be balanced by varying plants with different nutrient and root structure needs to maintain healthy soil. Beans and peas are legumes that fill the soil with nitrogen to become fertile for the next crop. Besides growing heavy feeders like corn and squash, legumes increase soil fertility and encourage better plant growth. Such natural nutrient cycling lessens the demand for synthetic fertilizers and contributes to a more sustainable gardening practice.

To do this, it is important to know the individual pest-repelling qualities of certain plants in relation to companion planting. For instance, marigolds have earned their reputations for repelling aphids, nematodes, whiteflies, etc. You can also plant marigolds around the gross or interspersed with your crops to create a barrier against these pests. Another versatile companion plant that repels mosquitoes and flies is basil. The strong scent of this plant confuses and deters these insects, and it's a good, scenting plant to plant nearby tomatoes and other susceptible crops.

Nasturtiums' role in companion planting is unique because they attract aphids away from the main crop. These colourful flowers sacrifice themselves for them and reel in aphids toward them rather than onto more valuable crops like cucumbers and beans. Garlic and onions have pungent ones that make them sturdy pest repellent. Planting garlic and onions near aphid-prone crops also helps protect them from aphid infestation. These alliums work as slug deterrents, too, and are notorious for destroying tender seedlings.

Companion planting combinations can make your garden a pest-free thriving habitat. One classic tomato, basil, and marigolds. The tomato flavour is improved by basil, which can also deter insects, and marigolds add a layer of pest protection. Other winners include carrots and onions. Onions repel the carrot fly, which can damage carrot roots, and carrots help to improve the soil structure of the onions. This trio is cabbage, dill with rosemary. Rosemary will deter cabbage moths and other weeds, while the dill will attract beneficial insects (ladybugs and parasitic wasps) all in one.

Traditional companion planting is a method known as the Three Sisters, which involves growing beans, corn, and squash together. Beans fix nitrogen in the soil, and squash shades the ground, suppressing weeds and retaining moisture. All three plants grow well together, stabilizing one another and providing a natural trellis for beans to climb to their height. With this proven method of companion planting, it is obvious why companion planting can help you grow a beautiful and bountiful garden.

Companion planting layout requires eyes when designing a plan. The intercropping techniques are where two or more different types of crops are planted together in the same joint to leverage the benefits of companion planting to the utmost. One example is planting lettuce between taller crop rows (tomatoes, peppers, etc.). The older lettuce can benefit from the shade provided by the taller plants as it keeps the soil warm and keeps the soil cool and moist. Another effective strategy is to create plant guilds and polycultures. Three Sisters is a plant guild, which are groups of plants that work well together. Growing a number of different crop types in the same place is referred to as a polyculture to increase biodiversity and reduce pest pressure.

Rotating companion plant placements each season helps maintain soil health and prevent the buildup of pests and diseases. Changing the location of your crops and their companions disrupts pest life cycles and reduces the risk of soil-borne diseases. Maintaining plant diversity throughout the garden is essential for a successful companion planting strategy. A diverse garden attracts a wide range of beneficial insects and creates a resilient ecosystem that can better withstand pest invasions.

Interactive Element: Companion Planting Layout Exercise

- **Assess Your Garden Space:** Sketch a map of your garden, noting the size and location of each bed.
- **Identify Key Crops:** List the main crops you plan to grow and their specific pest concerns.
- **Select Companion Plants:** Choose companion plants that benefit each crop, focusing on pest control and growth enhancement.
- **Plan Intercropping:** Determine which crops can be intercropped to maximize space and benefits.
- **Create Plant Guilds:** Group plants that work well together into plant guilds.
- **Rotate Placements:** Develop a plan for rotating companion plant placements each season.

Learning how to companion plant your vegetables is an easy way to boost their health and ensure they self-heal naturally and repel pests. This method improves your garden's productivity and contributes to an eco-friendly and sustainable way of handling pests. But with careful planning and the thoughtful selection of plants, you can have a thriving garden that requires less chemical intervention and supports a healthy ecosystem.

8.2 Natural Pesticides and Beneficial Insects

Using natural pesticides in your garden is like giving your garden a breath of fresh air. Chemical alternatives are invariably not as 'safe' for your plants, you, and the environment as natural pesticides. The chemicals that are reduced on crops lessen chemical residues in your food. It is important not to use chemicals; those chemicals protect beneficial insects and pollinators, like bees or butterflies. It removes the need to contaminate the soil and water, and that, in turn, is necessary for a healthy ecosystem. Plus, they help boost the garden's overall health and the biodiversity in your garden, making it a lively place. Making your natural pesticides at home is easy and effective. There is one recipe all those with one of these popular recipes out there use: neem oil for controlling aphids and spider mites. Mix two teaspoons of neem oil in 1 teaspoon of mild liquid soap and 1 quart of water to make neem oil spray. You can spray this mixture directly onto your plants' pests and forget about other beneficial insects. It is particularly good for organic gardeners who can let their pets benefit from neem oil; it is biodegradable and nontoxic to pets, birds, and other wildlife.

Garlic and chilli spray are other potent natural pesticides that repel various pests. To make this spray, puree two bulbs of garlic with water, let it sit overnight, strain the mixture, and add a tablespoon of chilli powder, a few drops of liquid soap, and more water to make a gallon. This potent concoction can be sprayed on your plants to deter insects like aphids, beetles, and caterpillars. It's a strong repellent, so handle it carefully to avoid contact with your skin and eyes.

This will work wonders for soft-bodied insects such as aphids, spider mites, and whiteflies, and it is simply soap and water spray. To this, put one and a half teaspoons of mild liquid soap and one quart of water. Apply this solution as a spray over the affected plants; it will also cover the underside of the leaves where these pests tend to go for refuge. The soap suffocates the insects without hurting your plants. However, be watchful not to use this spray in the hottest part of the day as it might damage your plants.

Your garden's little army of beneficial insects is crucial in natural pest control. For example, ladybugs eat voraciously on aphids. The Aphid Agrarian Society has determined that a single aphid can be consumed by up to 50 aphids every day, and they are essential allies. Another important asset is predatory wasps. Caterpillars foolishly host these tiny insects inside of them, which control their population with little effort. Tomato hornworms and cabbage loopers are pests that they are handy for.

Another beneficial insect to attract is lacewings. The larvae, or 'aphid lions' as they are often called, feed on aphids, mites, and other small insects. Indeed, hoverflies, which resemble small bees, are good pollinators, and the larvae of those hoverflies prey on aphids and other soft-bodied pests. What is done is encouraging these beneficial insects or other natural predators that will teach a natural balance in the garden and will be less chemical interventions necessary.

Growing beneficial insects is positive, as it increases population numbers to create habitats. But when it comes to gardens, insectary plants, like yarrow, fennel, and alyssum, help provide food and shelter for these helpful creatures. Nectar and pollen-producing plants are these plants that attract beneficial insects into your garden. For example, yarrow attracts predatory wasps, fennel and dill lacewings, and hoverflies.

A second step is providing water sources. Beneficial insects have a safe drinking spot within shallow dishes filled with water and pebbles. Insects can also be attracted to birdbaths, as they can be quickly moisturized without drowning there. You can help insect populations by building or installing insect hotels and shelters. Nesting sites and protection from the elements also encourage insect residence in your garden. Using materials such as bamboo, straw, or wood to build insect hotels quickly will create a cosy habitat for many beneficial insects.

Chemical pesticides have to be avoided to protect beneficial insects. Natural insecticides can be used sparingly and carefully. While these insects don't harm your flowers, overuse can damage the insects you wish to attract. Instead, plant and nurture a garden environment that encourages many beneficial insects. It also encourages a healthier, more balanced ecosystem that is more resilient to pests.

Your garden's natural pest control methods preserve it from nasty pests and allow it to flourish. They align with sustainable gardening rules and allow your garden to be productive for decades.

The next chapter will be devoted to growing your vegetables, the best types of vegetables to grow in confined spaces, and how to achieve the best possible harvest.

CHAPTER 9 GROWING VEGE-
TABLES

When I started growing vegetables in my small backyard, I wondered how to make the most of my limited space. It wasn't long before I realized that the key to a bountiful harvest lies in choosing the right plants and employing clever gardening techniques. If you're working with a small yard, balcony, or even just a few pots, there's no reason you can't enjoy a thriving vegetable garden. The trick is to focus on space-efficient gardening, which means selecting vegetables that grow well vertically and yield a lot per square foot.

9.1 Best Vegetables for Small Spaces

To get the most use out of your garden shape, be it on a small scale or in a very small setting, it is very important to select compact and vertical plants. Vegetable varieties that grow upwards instead of outwards take up less ground space and require less ground to cover. As well as increasing the height of the stem, this vertical growth also increases the air circulation, reducing the risk of disease and making harvesting easier. The other crucial factor is high-yield varieties. These plants are so generous, and in regard to their size, they are so bountiful. Ironically, they are so very generous that every square foot counts. Plants' compact and vertical growth leaves you with more space to grow plenty of plants and enjoy the harvest.

Leafy green choices for small gardens include lettuce, spinach, and kale. Multiple harvests throughout the growing season are a great perk; they grow quickly and do not need much space. Colder soils are better for lettuce and can be planted as a succession crop to keep the supply going. Another cool-season crop is spinach, which is rich in nutrients and will grow in partial shade. Kale is a cold, hardy vegetable with a great structure of leaves that can be harvested well into the fall.

Small space plants—regional varieties of bush beans and dwarf peas are the closest you will get to a gardener's secret. Bush beans, unlike their pole counterparts, are not heavy feeders and are compact enough to fit in constrained spaces. They yield a good harvest; they can be planted in succession and kept picking. Sweet-flavoured and tender pods and dwarf peas are other space-saving options. Growing them in containers is very easy, and they can even be trained to climb small trellises, which makes them very useful to maximize vertical space.

Any miniature garden must have cherry tomatoes and compact tomato varieties. They are bred to live in small spaces, fruiting loads with sweet and juicy fruits. In particular, curious are the other cherry tomatoes that can be grown in hanging baskets or pots. Determine and look for determinate or bush varieties that grow slower, stay smaller, and are less likely to overcome your space. Varieties like 'Tiny Tim' or 'Patio Princess' are excellent choices for container gardening.

Root vegetables do well in small gardens; radishes and baby carrots are favourites. Radishes are one of the quickest-growing vegetables, completing their growth within 3 weeks. It is perfectly used as filler between slower plants and can be harvested multiple times throughout the season. Baby carrots are ideal for container gardening as their root systems are short. Top varieties like 'Paris Market' are round and suitable for pots and raised beds.

Growing these vegetables in small spaces is successful if you start with a high-quality potting mix. The other mix should be rich in organic matter, allowing the nutrients to reach your plants. Drainage is very important when gardening in containers. The next step in maintaining appropriate vessel drainage is to ensure holes in your pots and planters are large enough to prevent over-watering, which can result in root rot. Implementing drip irrigation is a smart way to maintain consistent moisture levels. Drip systems also deliver water to the roots and help minimize waste.

To help their growth and production, your plants need to be fed with organic fertilizers. Pick a balanced fertilizer that offers all the required nutrients and feed it to your poinsettia regularly, as indicated in package directions. Growth and general plant health are enhanced with liquid seaweed fish emulsion.

Container and raised bed gardening are unique advantages to growing vegetables for gardening in small spaces. Container gardening powers are more precise than soil quality, sunlight, and growing conditions. Moreover, they are portable, so you may bring them to catch better light or save them from harsh weather. When picking containers, select pots of the appropriate size to grow the vegetables. The larger containers hold more soil, which keeps it wet and supports the infrequent need for water.

Another great option to use for small-space gardening is raised beds. Furthermore, they offer excellent drainage, help reduce the compaction of the soil, and improve the management of soil health. While your raised beds will still be sunlit, you may want to move them around to optimize their exposure for 6 to 8 hours of direct sun daily. Some other ways to maximize your growing area include vertical supports, such as trellises, with raised beds. A good example is climbing beans or cucumbers, which have space on a trellis where you can grow them rather than occupying ground space for other crops.

The management of soil health in confined spaces must be frequent. Add compost or organic matter to your soil during the planting season to add nutrients and structure. Mulching will help retain soil moisture, suppress weeds, moderate the temperature of the soil, etc. Take the time to inspect your plants for pests and diseases regularly and address the problem as soon as possible. Keeping an eye on these two factors will help you keep your small garden healthy and producing for the longest growing season.

Interactive Element: Small Space Gardening Checklist

- **Select Compact Varieties:** Choose vegetables that grow well in small spaces.
- **Use High-Quality Potting Mix:** Ensure your soil is rich in organic matter.
- **Ensure Adequate Drainage:** Use pots with drainage holes to prevent waterlogging.
- **Implement Drip Irrigation:** Maintain consistent moisture levels for your plants.
- **Feed Regularly:** Use organic fertilizers to support plant growth.

- **Maximize Vertical Space:** Use trellises and vertical supports to grow climbing plants.
- **Add Organic Matter:** Replenish soil nutrients each season with compost.
- **Mulch:** Retain moisture and suppress weeds with a layer of mulch.
- **Inspect Regularly:** Check for pests and diseases and take action as needed.

By selecting the right vegetables and employing clever gardening techniques, you can maximize your limited space and enjoy a thriving, productive garden. Whether growing in containers, raised beds, or a small patch of yard, these tips will help you succeed.

9.2 Companion Planting for Vegetable Gardens

A game changer for any vegetable garden is companion planning. Pairing plants strategically will help promote plant growth, decrease the number of pests, boost soil fertility, and increase biodiversity. This method ensures a mutual benefit between plants that strengthen each other by making healthier, more productive gardens. For example, some plants secrete chemicals that help grow other plants or supply shade or physical support to them. Companion planting has its own equally impressive natural pest deterrent. Some plants can repel harmful insects and thus make it convenient to lessen the use of chemical pesticides. In addition, companion plants can bring in nearby beneficial insects to help control pests and pollinate crops simultaneously. This effect is an overall improvement to your garden's resilience and encourages more balance in the ecosystem.

And to this day, two of the best-known companion pairings are tomatoes, basil, and marigolds. The pest-repelling properties of both basil and marigolds also benefit tomatoes. Sniffing Basil's strong scent like thrips and hornworms will die, marigolds repelling nematodes and aphids. Basil is also said to enhance tomatoes' flavour, which is a win-win. An effective alternative is to use carrots with onions and rosemary. Carrots also enrich the soil structure for the onions; indeed, onions release a sulfur compound that repels the carrot flies. Rosemary also aids in pest deterring as it provides a natural further layer of protection. The traditional Native American planting method in the Three Sisters combines beans, corn, and squash. Beans fix nitrogen in the soil, and with the natural trellis of corn growth, beans have an easy time climbing; squash helps the beans climb along it and spreads out to help suppress weeds while keeping the soil moist. As an example, this method demonstrates how one can create a self-sustaining ecosystem with companion planting. For pest control, cucumbers with radishes and nasturtiums are a good pairing. Radishes deter cucumber beetles; nasturtiums attract aphids from the cucumbers. With this combination, cucumbers will thrive but not be overrun by pests.

So planning a companion planting vegetable garden is a very important task. First, review your garden bed mapping to determine which companion pairs you'd like to use. Bring plants that help each other next to or adjacent to each other. Or, if you plant tomatoes and basil together, place the carrot and onion together in another. Companion plants must be rotated annually for healthy soil maintenance, and excess pests must be popped out. Alternating your companion pairs to different garden sections yearly will deplete the soil and disrupt pest cycles. Growing slowly and fast together, the intercropping techniques can help you make the best use of your space. Take tomatoes or beans growing between rows of tomatoes or beans, for example, and plant lettuce or radishes there. With this method, you put the productivity of your garden to its maximum extent and have a continuous harvest. A second tactic that works extremely well is using companion plants as natural pest barriers. Plant pest-repellent companions such as marigolds or onions around the edges of your garden beds to create a protective barrier. Not only does this deter pests, but it is also an attractive touch to your garden.

There are a number of examples of successful companion planting in real life. Consider an example of an urban gardener making over a small balcony garden by matching tomatoes with basil. My bountiful and healthy harvest resulted from tomatoes growing tall and basil warding off the pesky tomato borer. The urban setting did not restrict companion planting; the gardener proved how even the smallest spaces could be successful. A suburban homesteader is another inspiring case where a small plot of land was used to implement the Three Sisters method. In addition, this technique maximized the use of space and created a mini-ecosystem that needed little intervention. The bean grew on stalks of the corn, and the squash lay on the ground beneath it for a lush and productive garden.

Furthermore, companion planting has also had positive effects on the development of community gardens. A community garden was run into the ground by pests. They began planting vegetables as companions and tried some, such as marigolds and nasturtiums. It resulted in a marked decrease in vegetable pests and increased food production from vegetables. Unexpected benefits often come from personal anecdotes. One gardener found that planting cucumber with nasturtium deters pests and attracts more pollinators, thus helping the overall garden production.

There are numerous natural and effective ways, companion planting being one of them, to improve your vegetable garden. When choosing and pairing plants, you can maximize the results by avoiding competing plants from taking up space, watering, and nutrition. This method provides a balanced ecosystem, reduces the chemical treatment, and uses your little space. Companion planting requires some thought before it's put into use and proper implementation – but it can take your garden from blah to blooming in short order.

CHAPTER 10 GREENHOUSES AND HOOP HOUSES

The first time I walked into my greenhouse, it felt like stepping into another world. The warmth, the scent of damp earth, and the sight of thriving plants, even in winter, were magical. If you've ever dreamed of extending your growing season or protecting your plants from unpredictable weather, a greenhouse might be the solution you're looking for. Building a simple greenhouse can transform your backyard into a year-round garden, providing countless benefits beyond just growing vegetables.

10.1 Building a Simple Greenhouse

All that you can grow in a greenhouse regardless of the weather outside. Picture picking ripe tomatoes in the middle of January or harvesting fragrant herbs where the ground is solidly frozen. If we are talking about an extended growing season, you can try any variety of plants, including those that can't survive in your climate due to the lack of a proper growing season. Another feature of greenhouses is that they protect against frost and other extreme temperatures, such as harsh cold snaps or heat, which may affect your plants. In addition, you have more control over the growing conditions if you have a greenhouse. Essentially, you can regulate your temperature, humidity, and light levels, creating the perfect environment for your plants to grow, become healthier, and become more productive. A major advantage is that there is a lower pest and disease pressure. Its enclosed environment sheds many common garden pests, and although they do get in, it's easier to keep them out and manage what does get in, so it needs less chemical intervention.

Choosing the right place for your greenhouse is important for the success of the same. First, ensure a maximum amount of sunlight exposure. South-facing is best as it is the sun the plants will receive most during the daytime hours to give them the warmth and light needed to grow. Shades under tall buildings and trees should be avoided because they block the essential sunlight. Your greenhouse can also suffer from invasion of tree roots, which will compete with your plants for nutrients and water. You also want to be near enough to the water and electricity sources. If you're growing plants year-round, you'll also need the electricity to run heating and ventilation systems and easy access to water for irrigation. Protecting your greenhouse from strong winds is important as it can damage the structure or lower efficiency. If you can't find a way to protect the greenhouse from the wind, planting a row of shrubs or installing a fence will keep most of the wind at bay.

To build a simple greenhouse, you do not even need a contractor. Begin with selecting the material for the frame. PVC is the most widely used material because it is cheaper and easy to assemble but less durable than the alternative options. If you use rot-resistant types (cedar, redwood, or whatever), your wood will be more durable. All the other wood is said to make your house look charming and natural, but it might not be as tricky to rot or beat up as the alternatives. The best metal frames present are made from galvanized steel, making them very durable and very strong. However, these will cost more and take more time to assemble. After selecting your frame material, it is time to assemble the frame. You will tighten the frame by pressing it to the ground for the directives of choice material. For instance, this could involve concrete or stakes to keep the structure from moving or collapse in strong winds.

Next, install the greenhouse covering. Because polyethene is very affordable and easy to install, it is a common choice. It is lightweight and lets light through. However, it is prone to needing to be replaced every few years as it degrades over time. The polycarbonate panels are more durable and offer better insulation, so they are much better for those after a longer-term solution. However, glass is also the most expensive and fragile material because it is the most durable and aesthetically pleasing. Irrespective of whichever covering you choose, that covering needs to be snug on the frame, leaving room for ventilation, say, windows, vents, and fans. You need to keep good growing conditions by using proper ventilation while applying the growing mediums and preventing mould and overheating.

Keeping your greenhouse is necessary to keep it last and in good working condition. Clean the greenhouse covering regularly to allow maximum light penetration and prevent dirt or algae from accumulating. Check the structure regularly to inspect for any damage, such as cracks and loose connections, and fix them to avoid future issues. Maintaining humidity and ventilation for the plant is important. Mold and mildew will grow in the house if there is too much moisture and we cannot properly ventilate the room. Airflow is regulated, and the environment is kept stable with vents and fans. Seasonal tasks are also important. If you have a greenhouse in the summer, shading it will keep it from overheating. But in the winter, you can insulate it to keep your plants warm and protect them from frost.

Interactive Element: Greenhouse Maintenance Checklist

- **Clean Covering Regularly:** Remove dirt, algae, and debris to maintain light penetration.
- **Inspect for Damage:** Check for cracks, loose connections, and other structural issues.
- **Manage Humidity and Ventilation:** Vents and fans regulate airflow and prevent mould.
- **Seasonal Tasks:** Shade the greenhouse in summer and insulate it in winter to maintain optimal temperatures.

Building and maintaining a simple greenhouse can revolutionize your gardening experience, providing a controlled environment where plants can thrive year-round. Whether you're looking to extend your growing season, protect your plants from harsh weather, or experiment with new varieties, a greenhouse offers endless possibilities for enhancing your backyard homestead.

10.2 Utilizing Hoop Houses for Seasonal Extension

Hoop houses are an excellent addition to any backyard farm but a much cheaper, easier option than traditional greenhouses. Hoop houses are temporary structures that can be easily set up and taken down. They offer such flexibility regarding growing and can appeal to beginners and expert gardeners. You can specify the size and layout to fit your need of covering a small garden bed to a large area. Hoop houses are also very simple and, therefore, a great first step for someone starting with season extension techniques. Greenhouses can offer many of the same benefits as greenhouses but at a fraction of the cost and effort, and they provide many of these same benefits.

The little project of building a hoop house is a relatively straightforward weekend project. Start by selecting your materials. However, PVC pipes are used widely as PVC in pipes are affordable and easy to use. They are light to support structure and come with adequate strength. Metal hoops are durable and weather-resistant but require more effort to install. After choosing your materials, you will need to build the frame. Cut the PVC pipes or metal hoops to the length you want. For a standard garden bed, 10-foot pieces work very well. It is one of the easiest rebars to work with; drive the rebar into the ground at regular intervals along the length of your bed, keeping it parallel to run along. To form the arches, slip the rebar through the PVC pipes.

Later, put a greenhouse plastic or row covers over the frame. Row covers are lighter and allow more air circulation but are less durable than greenhouse-grade plastic. Both are excellent insulators. The covering is stretched over the frame so that it starts to prevent sagging. Clip it at the base or with stakes or heavy objects like bricks. End walls and doors can be added to help retain heat and be an easy access point. Wooden frames covered in plastic or premade end panels can be used. Make sure to include options for ventilation, like roll-up sides or vents to maintain temperature and humidity levels.

Especially shine for hoop houses, extending your growing season. Solar heat is trapped to provide a microclimate that is much warmer than that of the outside air. You can start earlier in the spring and keep your harvest going much longer. Hoop houses allow tender seedlings a better chance to survive when it gets cold and protect your plants from unexpected frosts. And they're also terrific for starting seeds ahead. Planting seeds in the hoop house and transplanting vigorous seedlings into the garden once the weather warms up is the best part of having a hoop house early in the season. Cold-hardy crops include spinach and kale, even in winter. Low-temperature tolerant plants are these plants, and the protection of a hoop house guarantees they continue to grow and produce throughout the season.

The hoop house is easy to maintain but needs regular attention to remain in good shape. There will be tiny holes in the covering, so start by checking them regularly. Have some repair tape for quick fixes, as small tears can become more visible and unaddressed. The structure must be secured against strong winds. Ensure the covering is nicely fastened and the frame appropriately anchored—Ventilate as weather changes. When warmer, open the sides or vents or seal them to stop the cold from coming in.

Snow accumulation is a concern in winter. Brush off any snow that has built up on the hoop house as regularly as possible because it will weigh it down and damage the structure. If the heaviest snow or ice is predicted, he will consider making the frame extra strong or temporarily removing the covering to avoid collapse. Perform a walk around of the whole structure, particularly after big weather events, on a monthly basis. Check for any loose connections, clogged drainage ditches, and other signs of damage, such as sagging. By taking these issues on quickly, your hoop house will stay a viable space to work in through the seasons.

The hoop house is a flexible, cost-effective method of boosting your backyard farming efforts. Manufacturer-supplied info: These structures are a practical solution accessible to gardeners, even those just starting, whether or not you would like to extend your growing season, protect tender plants, or start seeds early. Regular maintenance and some care will make your hoop house a valuable tool in your quest for a self-sufficient, year-round gardening life.

Ensuring your hoop house's longevity and efficacy is ensuring that you maintain it. Protecting your hoop house from the elements, regularly checking for damage, and readapting temperature to ventilation can keep your hoop house well cared for. By doing so, you will maintain your great ability to enjoy the advantages of enhanced growing season and protected plants to keep reaping the rewards of your backyard farm throughout the year.

Make a Difference with Your Review

Unlock the Power of Generosity

"The best way to find yourself is to lose yourself in the service of others." — Mahatma Gandhi

People who give without expecting anything back often live the happiest lives. That's why I'm asking for a small but powerful favor from you.

Would you help someone just like you—someone curious about backyard farming but unsure where to begin?

My goal is to make backyard farming fun, simple, and possible—even on less than an acre. But to reach more people who want to grow their own food and become more self-sufficient, I need your help.

Most readers pick a book based on reviews. So, by writing just a few kind words, you could help a future gardener start their journey.

Your quick review could help...

- ...one more family grow their own vegetables.
- ...one more beginner feel confident about starting.
- ...one more home become more sustainable.
- ...one more dream of self-sufficiency come true.

To make a difference, just scan the QR code below or visit:

https://www.amazon.com/review/review-your-purchases/?asin=B0F7XYKS3N

If you enjoy helping others, you're my kind of person.
Thank you so much for your support!

— **Cody Trent**

CHAPTER 11 HYDROPONICS SIMPLIFIED

One rainy afternoon, I stood in my kitchen looking at a bunch of wilted herbs I had picked from my garden. The constant battle with unpredictable weather and soil issues made me wonder if there was a better way to grow plants. That's when I stumbled upon hydroponics, a method that promised faster growth and higher yields without needing soil. Intrigued, I decided to try it, revolutionising my garden.

11.1 Basics of Hydroponic Systems

So, hydroponics is another method of planting plants, based on being fed by nutrient-rich water solutions and not on the soil. The plants get everything they need directly through the roots and grow faster, producing more in a single area. Hydroponics differs from traditional gardening as plants do not depend on soil to give them nutrients; they are all planted in a controlled environment. As this method is energy and time-efficient, it's very popular among home gardeners and commercial growers.

Hydroponics is an ancient practice. Early soil-less growing systems such as the Hanging Gardens of Babylon and the floating gardens of the Aztecs exist. With the onset of modern hydroponics in the early part of the twentieth century, scientists began to explore nutrient solutions. Since then, hydroponic techniques have evolved greatly. They are much more available and efficient. Hydroponics is used worldwide today to produce all kinds of crops, both greens and fruit producing.

Fast plant growth and high yield are regarded as one of the main reasons for using hydroponics. This means that in a hydroponic system, plants don't have to waste energy digging for their nutrients in the soil. Instead, they will have time to grow, maturing faster and harvesting more. Moreover, hydroponics allows one to control the nutrient levels, pH, and water quality to perfection to provide perfect conditions for growing. It also has space efficiency and is ideal for small gardens, urban spaces, and indoor use.

It is important to note several key differences between hydroponics and traditional soil-based gardening. Soil is a natural plant medium that harbours pests, diseases, and weeds. These issues are eliminated by hydroponics, where inert growing media, which again means that growing media fulfils all the functions as a carrier matrix in hydroponic culture, is not used, or none at all. Hydroponics systems deliver a balanced nutrient solution directly to the roots; the soil is also inconsistent with nutrient availability. Moreover, hydroponics uses less water than traditional gardening, as the closed systems reduce evaporation and runoff.

Hydroponic systems have numerous unique features and can be suitable or not suitable for certain types of plants. One of the simplest and most popular methods used is Deep Water Culture (DWC). The roots of plants dangle in a nutrient-rich water solution in a DWC system that is oxygenated by an air pump and air stone. It provides a constant supply of oxygen and nutrients, which provide a condition for rapid growth. DWC is just one form of DWC, but variations of DWC common in Northern climates include RDWC (recirculating DWC), regular DWC, and a convenient raft system, especially for leafy greens and herbs.

The nutrient film technique (NFT) implies a continuous flow of nutrient water over the roots of a crop. Sloped channels allow the water to flow through them, creating a thin film in which nutrients and oxygen are provided. .nsft systems are space efficient and work well for growing herbs and shallow-rooted vegetables such as lettuce and spinach. They can be designed vertically or horizontally, making them versatile and easy to use in any space. Despite being careful, the systems of NFT also require checking to prevent clogging and even nutrient distribution.

The other common type of hydroponic setup is drip systems. In such systems, the plants receive the nutrient solution from a network of tubes and emitters at the base of each plant. This is a precise watering and specific nutrient delivery control method, and as such, it is suitable for any plant, including larger plants such as tomatoes and peppers. Drip systems can scale well in small home gardens up to operation scale. Clogging and retained fertilizer prevent nutrient flow in any home hydroponics system, so regular maintenance is needed to keep these things in check.

Compared to hydroponics, aeroponics moves further by hanging the plant roots in the air and spraying the roots with the nutrient solution. Although it leads to rapid growth and high yields, this method gave maximum oxygenation. Aeroponic systems are more technically sophisticated, requiring more maintenance and using very little water. This method is often used for growing high-value crops and in research settings due to its precision and adaptability.

A hydroponic system is a relatively simple system and contains several basic components. The central hub is the reservoir that holds the nutrient solution. The material should be made of food grade one to avoid contamination. Pumps circulate the nutrient solution, and it gets to all the plants. An air pump and air stones are needed for systems like DWC to oxygenate the water so that root rot doesn't become a problem and healthy growth can occur. If growing trays or containers are used, they are grown in growing trays or containers and their growing medium.

They also reside in indoor hydroponic systems that use grow lights to supply sufficient light spectrum for photosynthesis. This is especially the case as LED grow lights are also very energy efficient and can emit specific wavelengths, which is important. In systems such as DWC and aeroponics, oxygenating the nutrient solution is crucial; air stones and pumps are essential. The lack of proper oxygenation is prone to the formation of anaerobic conditions that can cause root diseases and damage to the plant.

Preparing and maintaining the nutrient solution is vital for a successful hydroponic system. A wide range of available commercial nutrient mixes have been formulated to give various plant types balanced nutrition. These mixes have all the macromineral nutrients (nitrogen, phosphorus, potassium) and micromineral nutrients (magnesium, calcium, iron) a plant needs. If you are a DIY person, there are recipes online for nutrient solutions you can make and alter according to your plants' needs.

Hence, another major aspect of hydroponic gardening includes monitoring pH levels. In the plant, the pH of the nutrient solution also affects nutrient availability and plant health. A slightly acidic pH range of 5.5 to 6.5 is ideal for most plants' growth, and both pH meters and test kits are needed to test and adjust pH levels. You can increase pH by adding such substances as potassium hydroxide or decrease the pH by adding phosphoric acid. Regular monitoring makes sure that plants get a proper uptake of nutrients.

Water quality is equally essential in hydroponics. Filtered or distilled water is recommended to avoid contaminants affecting plant health. Tap water may contain chlorine, chloramine, or high levels of minerals that can interfere with nutrient absorption. Filters can remove these impurities, providing clean water for your hydroponic system. Regularly changing the nutrient solution, typically every two to three weeks, prevents the buildup of salts and ensures a fresh supply of nutrients.

Hydroponics offers a fascinating and efficient way to grow plants, making it accessible for those with limited space and a desire for self-sufficiency. By understanding the basics and setting up a reliable system, you can enjoy the benefits of faster growth, higher yields, and a more controlled growing environment.

11.2 Building Your Own Hydroponic Garden

Before choosing a location for your hydroponic garden, you need to plan it. Indoor setup is an option you may choose to have, with outdoor setups based on your space and particular needs. Controlled environments make regulating temperature, light, and humidity easier with indoor gardens. However, this growth is controlled and can be consistent; it is just a situation of having adequate space and growing lights. Natural sunlight is easier to achieve outdoors, and artificial lighting sometimes does not need to be utilized; however, it can also be exposed to weather and pests. Deciding this depends on your climate and the space available.

Once you determine your location, you can look at the space and layout available. Calculate the area you will use it and sketch a simple design. It lets you see where each component will go, such as the reservoir, growing trays, and any necessary pumps or tubing. Stacking growing trays or wall-mounted systems can also use space above the ground in smaller areas. Depending on your space dimensions, this will help you choose the right hydroponic system and its components.

For success, selecting plants that thrive in hydroponic systems is important. For beginners, leafy greens such as lettuce, spinach, and kale grow fast, yet the nutrient requirement is relatively low. Basil, mint, and cilantro also grow well in hydroponics. You can also go more adventurously and start fruiting plants like tomatoes, peppers, and strawberries with similar fantastic results. Explore each plant's unique requirements and ensure that they will work with what your hydroponic system can offer.

Thus, lighting is another important factor. Hydroponic gardens may be set up inside the office walls, but they rely on grow lights to provide the needed light, as plants require it for photosynthesis. Such LED grow lights are popular because they are energy efficient and can be created to produce specific light spectrums. Determine the amount of light your plant needs by considering its intensity and how long it needs a light. All plants need a minimum of 12 to 16 hours of light daily. Keep the grow lights at the right angles of the plants to prevent burning or inadequate exposure to light.

Gather the needed materials and tools to construct your hydroponic system. For a basic, cheap DWC, you will need a reservoir with a plastic tote, air pump, air stones, net pots, and a medium such as clay pebbles. To start, create holes for the net pots to sink into the reservoir lid. Add the air stones to the bottom of the reservoir and connect them to the air pump. Fill the reservoir and add in the nutrient solution. Locating the net pots with seedlings into the holes and dropping the seedlings into the holes drip with nutrient water effectively concludes a nutrient-rich cycle.

For a Nutrient Film Technique (NFT) system, you will need channels (PVC pipes or gutters), a water pump, tubing, and a reservoir. Put the channels aside enough so the nutrient solution covers the roots as they flow over them. Put the water pump in the reservoir and send the nutrient solution with tubing to the channels' tops. A solution cycle will flow down the channels back into the reservoir. Plant the plants in a net pot and put them into holes along the channels, kindly so that the roots touch the flowing nutrient solution.

The other versatile option is drip systems. A drip system will require a reservoir, a water pump, tubing, drip emitters, and growing containers. Put the containers down onto a flat surface and tube from the reservoir to each container. At the end of each tube, a drip emitter is installed to control the flow of the nutrient solution. The solution will be pushed through the tubing from the water pump directly to the base of each plant. Monitoring the plant's uptake of water and nutrients can be controlled with this method with high accuracy.

Some care is required when starting seeds or seedlings of a hydroponic system. The first step is to germinate seeds in a moist environment, e.g., on a damp paper towel, until they sprout. However, instead of using the potting tray, you can do it in seedling trays with a growing medium, like Rockwool or Coco Coir. At the next stage, when the seeds have grown true leaves, transplant them into the hydroponic system. Roots should be in touch with the nutrient solution, but the plant shouldn't be submerged to prevent stem disease.

It is crucial to monitor and adjust nutrient levels. Check the nutrient concentration in the solution regularly using an electrical conductivity (EC) meter. The solution should be diluted with water if the EC levels are too high. If the values are too low, you should add more nutrients. Also, the pH of the plants should be monitored and kept at optimal levels, usually between 5.5 and 6.5. Experiment with the pH up or down solutions to adjust pH levels.

Pruning and training growth help optimize yields. Pull off dead or yellow leaves frequently to encourage healthy growth and fight disease. Vining plants such as tomatoes, stakes, or trellis support the stems to guide growth. Pruning and training ensure good airflow and light in all parts of the plant, thus resulting in more abundant harvests.

Part of maintaining a healthy garden is troubleshooting common hydroponic issues. Discoloured leaves, stunting of growth, and the like are other ways nutrient deficiencies manifest. To do this, alter the nutrient solution and maintain the correct pH. Exposing the actual water also blocks the light, which can cause algae growth and root rot. In addition, the water requires sufficient oxygenation to prevent rot. Natural remedies like neem oil or insecticidal soap can control pests and diseases in the indoor system. Keep a regular eye on your plants and system components for such issues.

Interrupting your hydroponic system can occur through equipment failure – such as pump failure or clogged tube. Regular maintenance checks and cleaning prevent these problems. Have spare parts ready so that replacement of faulty components can be quick. If you wish your hydroponic garden to stay consistent, proactive maintenance will ensure it.

If you want to enjoy the advantages of quicker growth and higher yields of hydroponic gardens, you must plan well, set up the right system, and maintain it accordingly. This method is reasonable for anyone with little space but gives you a controlled environment for successful plant growth. The next chapter will tell you about the world of perennial crops, fruit trees, and berry bushes that can enrich your backyard farm.

CHAPTER 12 FRUIT TREES
AND BERRY BUSHES

Consider a hot summer day in your greenhouse; you open the door and breathe that cool air. The air may be cool, the plants may thrive, and no mould or pests will be present. Enough ventilation is required to achieve this ideal environment. A healthy greenhouse depends on proper airflow. It helps your plants to have the fresh air they need, controls temperatures and prevents diseases. So why is ventilation important, and how do you create a system that will work for you?

12.1 Dwarf and Semi-Dwarf Fruit Trees

Ventilation in a greenhouse is not just about opening a window. The idea is that everything has to be created with an environment where plants can breathe, grow, and resist diseases. If greenhouses have no airflow, they can become too hot very quickly. In excess, heat can stress the plants, causing wilting and even death. This prevents heat buildup by circulating air so your plant isn't getting too hot. Thus, your plant will be kept at a stable temperature.

Humidity is another critical factor. Gives mold and mildew to the plant and can devastate the whole plant. This helps lower these moisture levels and creates a drier, healthier environment. Aside from this, plants also need carbon dioxide for photosynthesis. In an enclosed space, growth can be stunted due to CO_2 levels dropping. Fresh air is brought in, which replenishes CO_2 and guarantees that plants have what they need to do well. Good airflow also minimizes pest problems. Having stagnant air makes your greenhouse more inviting to many of these pests, so keeping the air moving will keep it less inviting to most of them.

To design an effective ventilation, you have to know its key components. Roof vents are essential. This way, they let hypodermic air get away from the height of the greenhouse as it rises by nature. Sidewall vents work with roof vents by bringing in cooler, fresh air from outside. This results in a flow that forces hot air out and pulls cold air in, and exhaust fans are also essential. To cope even when natural ventilation isn't adequate, they continuously move air out of the greenhouse, maintaining the airflow. Circulation fans finish by helping circulate the air in the greenhouse so that hot spots don't develop and circulation throughout the space is kept even with regard to temperature and humidity.

Select the appropriate size and number of vents if you need some fans. For your roof and sidewall vents combined, the area should total about 20% of the greenhouse floor area. This ensures adequate airflow. Position your fans strategically. For intake vents or fans, you should put them lower; for exhaust fans, you should place them high up on the walls, roof, or any other place to remove the hot air. Integrate automatic vent openers. These handy devices close (or open) vents depending on the temperature inside the greenhouse and thus give consistent ventilation, freeing you from the job of constant monitoring. Plan for cross-ventilation. Make sure that air can move from side to side inside the greenhouse; it will make your ventilation system more effective.

Ventilation systems can be controlled with automated systems that will take your greenhouse to the next level. These systems have sensors that automatically monitor temperature and humidity and change vents and fans to keep conditions at the optimum level. Temperature and humidity sensors supply real-time temperature and humidity data, making it possible for the system to respond rapidly to the changes. To prevent overheating your greenhouse, your automated vent openers can be set to open when temperatures rise. Fans receive programmed timers that enable you to program specific times for ventilation to ensure a constant environment without any manual adjustments. These elements are all taken in by the innovative greenhouse control systems that allow you to control your greenhouse's climate from one interface, sometimes via a smartphone.

If you do not design your greenhouse for ventilation, you don't understand how your plants will thrive. Proper airflow will stop the heat buildup, lower the humidity, allow carbon dioxide exchange, and, most importantly, minimize pest problems. The roof vents, sidewall vents, exhaust, and circulation fans constantly supply fresh, healthy air. Automated systems eliminate much guesswork in keeping the perfect greenhouse climate; you can improve efficiency and consistency. This is why many people opting for an alternative greenhouse, like a small patio greenhouse or a homesteader with a bigger setup, will want to invest in a sound ventilation system for a bountiful, healthy garden.

Visual Element: Ventilation System Layout Guide

A typical greenhouse layout may be included here, along with a diagram showing the placement of roof vents, side-wall vents, exhaust fans, and circulation fans. This visual can assist the readers in placing each component in an appropriate position to get the best air circulation.

12.2 Natural Ventilation Methods

Imagine a greenhouse itself innovating, where there is no need for mechanical intervention regarding how naturally the air flows and the temperature is maintained throughout. The promise of natural ventilation is this. Passive airflow can help you create a cost and energy-efficient greenhouse environment. Natural ventilation is a way of using wind and buoyancy to move air through your greenhouse. Relying less on mechanical systems, such a configuration reduces energy costs and makes it more sustainable. It is a method that saves money and protects the growing environment by providing healthier conditions than natural ones.

Installing roof vents is one of the simplest ways to help natural ventilation. The hot air that rises naturally escapes from the top of the greenhouse and is allowed through roof vents. This method helps keep the place cool, especially during the hotter months. The second is another practical solution – roll-up sidewalls. Rolling up the sides of your greenhouse will create adjustable airflow that allows cool breezes in while exhausting warm air out. This technique is necessary for hoop houses or other temporary improvements where flexibility is crucial. Vent windows provide targeted ventilation, and opening certain parts will help send what is needed to the place where it is needed the most. Secondly, positioning your greenhouse doors with a cross breeze improves overall airflow. If the end objective is to maximize natural air movement through the structure, then aligning doors on opposite sides of the greenhouse is a good way.

Setting up is very important to achieve optimal natural ventilation. Your first step should begin as you turn your greenhouse to receive prevailing winds. When you put the greenhouse in position, avoid the wind winds running up the sidewalls, increasing the natural ventilation effect. Shading can also help in reducing the heat within the greenhouse. Shade cloth can keep the interior cooler, or strategically placed plants can block them. It is also importanti to ensure unobstructed airflow paths. Set up your runs to avoid places where large objects or dense plantings will get in the way of ventilation routes. In doing so, air is given the necessary freedom and efficiency to move about. A key factor in balancing the size and the location of your vents. Your roof and sidewall vents must be appropriately sized and positioned so that air will pass through the greenhouse constantly.

Natural ventilation has many benefits, but some limitations should be aware of. In addition, there is a big obstacle in controlling the airflow. In contrast to mechanical systems, natural ventilation does not rely on internal factors alone but on external ones: wind and thermal gradients. During calm weather, when no wind drives the airflow, the result is inconsistent ventilation. A drawback is that an increased risk of pest entry exists. Easy access to insects and other pests can be obtained through open vents and sidewalls. This is not to say that using fine mesh screens will prevent this completely, but you can think of it. Natural ventilation is additionally affected by seasonal changes. In colder times, you may need to rely more on mechanical systems to keep the temperature at suitable levels because natural ventilation alone may not be enough to warm.

Dealing with these challenges will enable you to maximize the natural ventilation of your greenhouse. This is a way to grow that, properly used, can provide a durable and economical growing environment.

12.3 Combatting Mold and Mildew

Imagine instantly walking into your greenhouse and seeing mould spread across your plants. Sadly, it's a common problem that gardeners face. Areas with high humidity, poor circulation, and surface condensation are warm and hostile to mould and mildew. Thus, under these conditions, these non-wanted fungi get the perfect breeding ground to infect the plant and cause plant stress and diseases. Mould can starve plants of sunlight and inhibit photosynthesis, while mildew will cause the leaves to discolour and die eventually. The problem can spread fast; it's essential to attack it aggressively.

High humidity levels are one of the main villains that cause mould and mildew. When the air in your greenhouse is too moist, it is a ready and safe environment for fungal spores. This problem worsens with poor air circulation because moisture will be drawn to plant surfaces and other areas. Mold has a better chance of materializing when the surface condensates, particularly on colder nights. Stress happens over time, weakening plants' defences and leaving their structures soft and prone to diseases. To avoid this, ventilation has to be maintained properly. It helps prevent humidity and guarantees fresh air throughout the greenhouse.

Maintaining a good humidity level is dependent on dehumidifiers in some ways. Removing surplus humidity from the air helps create an unfriendly environment for mould and mould. Another one is implementing regular cleaning routines. Take clean surfaces, tools, and containers regularly to remove spores that may be lurking. This reduces the chances of a mould starting to take root. It's also essential to have enough space between plants. The closed, crowded plants can trap moisture and restrict airflow, trapping high-humidity pockets of mould growing. Proper plant spacing helps the air circulate better and reduces the possibility of fungal growth.

Early detection is vital if mould and mildew are found. Symptoms to look out for are white or grey fuzz on leaves, discoloured patches, and a musty smell. Acting quickly if you see these signs will help to stop the problem from worsening. If there is an affected part of the plant, remove it and dispose of it away from the greenhouse. It contains the spread of spores. Organic fungicides may also be applied. Neem oil is an alternative because of its antifungal properties. Spray on the affected areas and mix with water. Another option is baking soda sprays. Bake with water and liquid soap, mix with baking soda, and apply to mouldy areas. The two treatments work by altering the pH of the plant surface to make it not inhospitable to mould.

Increasing airflow and reducing humidity are crucial steps in combating mould. Use fans to keep the air moving, and ensure your ventilation system works efficiently. Sometimes, opening vents or doors can help lower humidity and improve air circulation. Regular monitoring is essential. Conduct frequent inspections to catch any signs of mould early. Adjust your ventilation settings as needed based on the conditions inside the greenhouse. Cleaning and disinfecting surfaces regularly can prevent mould from taking hold. Use a solution of water and vinegar or hydrogen peroxide to wipe down surfaces. This not only kills spores but also deters their return.

Keeping detailed records of humidity levels and plant health can be beneficial. Note any environmental or plant behaviour changes, and adjust your maintenance routines accordingly. This proactive approach allows you to spot trends and address issues before they become significant problems. Remember, prevention is always better than cure. Maintaining a clean, well-ventilated greenhouse and monitoring conditions closely can keep mould and mildew at bay, ensuring your plants remain healthy and productive.

Effective mould and mildew control creates an environment that doesn't support fungal growth. Proper ventilation, humidity control, and cleanliness are your best defences. Regular monitoring and maintenance are crucial to catching problems early and preventing recurrence. With these strategies, you'll be well-equipped to maintain a healthy, thriving greenhouse.

CHAPTER 13 HERBS AND
SPICES

I had a handful of fresh basil I wished for when preparing homemade pasta sauce for one summer evening. Unfortunately, store-bought dried herbs weren't cut. It was at that time I decided to start growing my culinary herbs. It was not only an incredible flavour to my dishes, but it also changed the way I cook and garden. It doesn't matter how small your space is; growing culinary herbs at home has a lot of benefits and will be a rewarding project for any homeowner, homesteader, or gardener.

13.1 Essential Culinary Herbs

Growing culinary herbs at home is one of the easiest and most rewarding things to do with gardening. These herbs flavour your dish and save you greatly over buying fresh at the store. If you grow them indoors, you still have access to fresh ingredients; however, you have them year-round. Fresh herbs are also worthwhile in terms of health benefits, as they are rich in important vitamins, minerals, and antioxidants that aid in overall well-being. A supply of fresh herbs right at your fingertips can stimulate you to cook and invent wonderful-tasting food that is also healthy.

And when picking culinary herbs, there are a few key ones for quick success in the kitchen. Basil is a warm-season herb and only survives during the summer months. It's a bright, aromatic leaf with which a person can make pesto, garnish salads and salads, and add to Italian dishes. Basil likes full sun and well-drained soil, which can be grown in the garden or pots. You will need parsley, a biennial herb with a crisp and slightly peppery taste. It is used as a garnish but is also good for use with other herbs in salads or sauces. This plant grows best in full sun to partial shade and waterlogged soil.

Thyme is another herb that makes it worth having in your garden. This robust, earthy herb is a perennial that is an ideal addition to soups, stews, and roasted meats. Drought tolerant and flourishing in well-drained soil with lots of sunlight, thyme is one you've got a lot to gain for just a minimal investment of effort in their care. Like rosemary, it is a perennial herb frequently used in roasted vegetables, grilled meat, braised foods, and wine. It can be grown both indoors and outdoors, and it is drought-tolerant. Rosemary requires full sun and well-drained soil; the leaves are most easily harvested when used, but the plant is ever-green and can be cut year-round.

Growing culinary herbs both indoors and outdoors is fairly simple. Selecting the right containers and soil mix is always a start. Well-draining soil is something most herbs dislike, and to remedy this situation, consider a mix specifically made for herbs or amend a general-purpose potting mix with sand or perlite. Ensure your containers have drainage holes to avoid waterlogging, which can kill them with root rot. Idcally, your herbs should be placed where they receive sun for 6-8 hours daily. Indoor herbs are grown best in a sunny windowsill or under grow lights.

Watering is another aspect of herb care. Soil is mostly moist but not waterlogged; most herbs prefer this soil type. Water your herbs when the surface of the soil is 1 inch down, and the top of the root system feels dry, and don't get the foliage wet to prevent fungal diseases. Fertilizing herbs can also promote healthy growth if they are used with organic, herb-specific fertilizers. Use the fertilizer package instructions, usually four to six times per season.

Growing culinary herbs keeps them continuously growing, and has the best flavour if harvested immediately. For basil, pinch off the top leaves occasionally as they grow to make them bushier and prevent the plant from growing into a flower, making the leaves bitter. Cut the parsley stems at the base, from which new growth will shoot out from the plant's interior. To harvest thyme at its best, do it just before it flowers when its flavour is strongest. When making needed sprigs, cut a third or a little more than a third of the plant at a time, but avoid cutting back more than snip sprigs of thyme needed. Year-round, the Rosemary can be cut back, whenever needed, into sprigs for snipping off. It is easy to eat any time of the day as its stems are very sturdy.

Growing your culinary herbs in containers will allow you to have fresh, flavorful ingredients right at your fingertips when making meals for a healthier lifestyle. It is often easier to readily have herbs as they allow you to try new recipes and elevate your everyday meals. Whichever herbs you have or choose to cultivate—whether in a sprawling garden or pots on the windowsill—the joy of gardening and cooking is united in cultivating herbs, which is rewarding.

13.2 Growing and Preserving Spices

The way to spoil yourself with spices is to grow them yourself at home, which is also how to wean yourself from buying spices repeatedly. Think of sitting and enjoying the aroma of homegrown coriander seeds or freshly dried cumin powder in your hand to add to your dishes. It then brings homegrown spices to your meals, giving you a personal touch and the opportunity to explore some exotic and rare varieties that might not be available in the supermarket. Moreover, spices can also be enjoyable to grow, and there is nothing more adventurous than making homemade preserves and pickles with new flavours to liven up your culinary adventures.

The reward of growing a spice garden filled with spices for specific cooking cuisines is one. Both an annual herb and a spice, coriander is an annual herb whose seeds are used. It's used in many Indian, Middle Eastern, and Mexican dishes. Growing coriander from seed is easy, and the plant grows readily in full sun and well-drained soil. Once or twice a week, sprinkle the seeds on the surface of the bed or container, keeping the soil moist until germination, then thin the seedlings to 2-4 inches apart.

Cumin is another excellent spice to grow at home. It is a warm-season annual with aromatic seeds, a principal flavouring term in many spice blends and dishes. It grows well in sandy soil in the sun. Plant seeds indoors a few weeks before the last frost date to emerge the seedlings and transplant when the weather warms. Cumin plants need regular watering but shouldn't be overwatered as they are prone to root rot.

Fennel is a perennial herb, and its seeds and bulbs are used in culinary ways. Internally, the seeds are used for baking, spice blends, and tea, and the bulb is roasted or added to salads. Although fennel thrives in full sun and well-drained soil, it will grow in partial sun or shade and rocky places. They can be grown from seed, but the best results will be from seedling transplants. Plant the plants about 12 inches apart so they will have room to grow, and water regularly to keep the soil moist.

Another easy-to-growing mustard plant should be added to the list: the mustard plant. The seeds of this annual plant are used for making mustard sauce or spice blends. Because it requires full sun and moderately fertile, well-drained soil, mustard can only grow well in that preferred soil. Spread the seeds in the garden bed or container and thin out the seedlings to around 6 inches apart. When keeping the soil moist but not waterlogged, watch out for pests such as aphids and flea beetles.

Cultivating spices in containers and garden beds requires some practical considerations. For containers, choose deep ones for the rooting systems of your spice plants. Coriander and cumin can be planted in pots 8-10 inches deep, whereas fennel may require bigger containers. Healthy spice plants are exacting when it comes to soil preparation. For fertility, add organic matter like compost to the well-draining potting mix.

Another important factor for the growth of spice is sunlight. Almost allspice plants need full sun, that is, a minimum of six hours of direct sun daily. For herbs growing indoors, they might need as much light as possible, preferably a south-facing window, or grow lights should be used if not. Water is just as important to keep the soil moist, but not too much, as you don't want to cause root rot or other problems. Keep an eye on your plants, look for pests and diseases, and do something about them if you spot any. Common pests can be controlled using such natural remedies as neem oil or insecticidal soap.

Once you have successfully grown your spices, you will be assured of a supply throughout the year so long as you learn how to preserve the spices. Preserving coriander seeds is a simple and very effective air-drying process. When the seed turns brown, harvest and dry it in a warm, dry place; keep the dried seeds in airtight containers to keep the flavour and potency as they were. Grounding cumin seeds and toasting them can also help them taste better. Heat a dry skillet over medium heat, add the seeds, and toast until fragrant. Grind the seeds into powder only after they cool down.

Also, fennel seeds can be harvested and dried the same way. If the seed heads turn brown perfectly, cut them and put them in a paper bag. Place the bag in a warm, dry place and hang it until the seeds have dehydrated. Preserve the flavour of the fennel seeds by storing them in airtight containers. Another rewarding activity is to make homemade mustard out of harvested mustard seeds. Mustard seeds are ground into a powder and mixed with vinegar, water, and spices to make a tasty mustard sauce.

Growing and preserving your spices allows you to enjoy the rich, authentic flavours only fresh spices provide. This practice enhances your culinary creations and connects you to the food production process, fostering a deeper appreciation for the ingredients you use. Whether you have a large garden or a small balcony, spice gardening offers endless possibilities for adding unique flavours to your kitchen.

CHAPTER 14 CHICKENS IN
YOUR BACKYARD

On a nice morning one day ago, my porch coffee already consumed, I heard a pleasant clucking sound. To my surprise, my newly acquired chickens were scratching the ground and foraging for bugs. The sight was mesmerizing. I had never considered raising chickens a conveniently manageable undertaking suitable for someone with a backyard. These feathered friends weren't pets but the newest contributors to our homestead's self-sufficiency.

14.1 Selecting the Right Chicken Breeds

Becoming their backyard chickens' proud owners and raisers might have more advantages than just some fresh eggs. Chickens can kill pests naturally by eating insects and weeds that might harm your garden. Also, their droppings are rich in nutrients and can be composted to make a fantastic fertilizer for your soil. Furthermore, chickens offer limitless entertainment and company; you can't beat them as a livable addition to a homestead. However, before you choose which chicken breeds to select, consider a few factors to fit your and their environment correctly. Climate adaptability is crucial. Both breeds are cold hardy for those living in cold regions.

On the other hand, if you live in the warmer part of the world, the Leghorn or Silkie may be a better choice as they are good at tolerating heat. The other critical factor is egg production. Rhode Island Reds are also hardy and prolific egg layers, putting as many as 300 large brown eggs on the shell yearly. However, if you want a friendly and good-with-family breed, Buff Orpington has a friendly temperament suitable for families.

Space requirements are also a large consideration. Bantam breeds are small-sized and need less space, but they are suitable for small-sized areas. For example, if the Silkie is one of your bantam breeds, it can live in smaller coops. Necessary amounts of room were not created for the larger standard-sized breeds like the Rhode Island Red and Plymouth Rock, which sometimes boasted higher egg production, along with the dual-purpose production of eggs and meat.

The Rhode Island Red is among the popular chicken breeds for backyard flocks because it is robust and highly egg-producing. They are an all-around sturdy, adaptable, hardy breed suited to cool and warm climates. Another favourite breed is the Buff Orpington due to its friendliness and suitability for families. This breed can be cold-hardy and lays a moderate amount of medium-brown eggs. The Plymouth Rock has its striking all-black and white plumage with its eggs and meat, making it a dual-purpose breed. Bearded Red Cape provides a hardy nature and gentle temperament that is great to put into any backyard flock.

Famous for its excellent laying ability, the Leghorn produces many white eggs and is heat-tolerant for warmer climates. Last, the Silkie is a bantam breed with fluffy plumage, a calm demeanour, and laying creamy-coloured small to medium eggs. They are known for their broody nature and make good mothers if you plan on hatching chicks.

Sourcing chickens is not an easy task; you have a few options. The best way to acquire birds is from reputable hatcheries — you do not know what you will get, and it is possible to get very unhealthy birds that do not have a known bloodline. Murray McMurray Hatchery has online hatcheries where you can purchase various breeds and get detailed information about the breed to make an educated decision. Chickens may be found at local farms and feed stores, where they can be seen before you buy them. In addition, there are organizations offering chicken rescue and adoption, where birds can find new homes to be given to. It can be very rewarding.

There are others to consider when buying chicks versus adult hens. Chicks are a bit more work in their early days, but they bring you close to them early on. Additionally, they are usually less expensive. Indeed, adult hens are already laying and do not require much initial care, making them ideal for people who want a quick egg click.

Interactive Element: Chicken Breed Selection Guide

To help you decide which chicken breeds are best suited for your backyard, consider the following checklist:

- **Climate:** Is your area predominantly hot, cold, or moderate?
- **Egg Production:** How many eggs per week do you need?
- **Temperament:** Do you have children or pets that will interact with the chickens?
- **Space:** How much space can you allocate for your chickens?

- **Purpose:** Are you interested in dual-purpose breeds for eggs and meat?

After thinking carefully about these factors and choosing appropriate breeds, a healthy backyard flock can be formed featuring fresh eggs, assisting in pest control and soil health, and making your homestead a joy to be in. Raising chickens can be a fun and fruitful experience that would bring practical benefits and some rustic feel to your backyard.

14.2 Building a Chicken Coop

The most important aspect of having an adequate home for your chickens is to make it a safe, functional, & comfortable place for your chickens to live and thrive. There are several key requirements that a well-designed chicken coop answers. Firstly, space is paramount. Each chicken should have enough roosting, nesting, and space to walk around. The aim should be at least 3-4 square feet per chicken inside the coop and 4 square feet per chicken in the outdoor run. It is also essential to avoid respiratory problems by having adequate ventilation. But ensure your coop has ventilation or windows that let fresh air circulate while keeping the drafts at bay. More importantly, it protects against predators. Securing secure latches and hardware cloth prevents unwanted visitors from entering the area. Also, the last important thing is ease of cleaning and maintenance. An easy-to-clean coop will help your chickens to stay healthy and keep your job easy.

It is rewarding to build your chicken coop. First of all, you need to make the right choice of materials. The wood is a popular choice as it is readily available and easy to work with. Untreated wood may avoid chemical exposure to the chickens. The coop can also be put together from metal, which can be used for the roof, for example, to add some extra durability. Hardware cloth is recommended for predator-proofing because it's stronger than chicken wire. Construct the frame of the coop, beginning with a sturdy base and frame of 2x4s, according to the dimensions your flock needs. Attach the walls once the frame is complete using plywood or similar material. Always leave openings for the doors and windows.

After that, install the nesting boxes and roosting bars. Put the nesting boxes in a quiet, dimly lit coop area to give privacy to your hens. Usually, only one nesting box per three hens is required. It must be such that the boxes are easily accessible to the chickens and for egg collection. The roosting bars should be different heights and have about 8 inches of space per chicken. To be used, install these bars at least 2 feet off the ground to provide a comfortable resting place. It is also necessary to add doors and windows to the coop. Make sure the doors are large enough for easy passage to wash and maintain. Hardware cloth, which should be covered over windows to keep predators out but permit ventilation, should be used to cover the windows.

Construction of the coop naturally involves thoughtfully designing the interior layout. The simplest method is to place the nesting boxes lower than the roosting bars and discourage the chickens from sleeping in them. This prevents the nesting boxes from becoming messy when the egg is laying. Place waterers and position feeders (as possible) in an accessible area, but not in the roosting area, to reduce droppings contamination. Provide dust bath areas for chickens to control parasites such as mites and lice by incorporating them into your coop or run. You can create a dust bath in a shallow box or container by putting sand, wood ash, and diatomaceous earth into it.

However, like any other environment, the coop needs constant cleaning and attention to detail; otherwise, it becomes unhealthy. Form daily and weekly routines to remove droppings, change soiled bedding, and deep clean for weekly routines. To keep in a clean environment, use a straw, wood shavings, or other absorbent bedding that should be changed regularly. It is extremely important to prevent mite and lice infestations. Check on your chickens periodically for pests, and if you need to, treat your chicken coop with natural remedies such as diatomaceous earth. You also need to make seasonal adjustments for the flock to be comfortable. Insulate the coop in the winter to conserve heat and not have your water ice. During the summer, give shade and ventilation for their coop to remain cool.

Following these guidelines will create a chicken coop to meet your flock's needs and boost their health and productivity. All this means that your coop will be well maintained, which is essential for happy and healthy chickens contributing to a thriving homestead.

Now that your coop is built and your flock has settled, you are on your way to reaping the benefits of backyard chicken raising. Second, I will take you on a journey into seed selection and saving the world so your garden keeps producing year after year.

⮵

CHAPTER 15 SEED SELECTION AND SAVING

Once, on a spring afternoon, I encountered a stall selling heirloom seeds while going through the local farmers' market. I was curious about the colourful packets and the unusual vegetables they promised, so I approached the vendor. It explained the importance of heirloom seeds, passing them down through generations to keep the plant and the people who grew them. The seeds of this encounter ignited my instinct for figuring out and opting for top seeds, as they are one of the fundamental needs for any gardener aiming at having a successful and enduring backyard farmer.

15.1 Understanding Seed Types

The base of a successful garden is choosing the right seeds. If you've heard terms like hybrid, heirloom, and open-pollinated thrown around, you might wonder what they mean. Creating hybrid seeds is crossbreeding two different parent plants to create a seed with some desirable traits. Some of these traits might be resistance to disease uniformity with higher yields. Seeds of hybrid plants may produce true-to-type plants in the next generation. However, seeds saved from these plants are more likely to produce plants that do not display the same qualities as their parent plants.

On the other hand, heirloom seeds are open-pollinated varieties passed down from generation to generation for at least 50 years. These seeds' flavour, genetic diversity, and historical significance make them so cherished. Heirloom seeds are open-pollinated, meaning if the Emerald plants are not swerving by the company, they get cross-pollinated, producing plants very similar to parent plants. This ability to produce similar plant characteristics year after year makes them useful for seed savers.

Open-pollinated seeds are pollinated by nature, i.e. insects, birds, wind, or other natural means. All the heirloom seeds are open-pollinated, but not all open-pollinated seeds are heirlooms. The advantage of open-pollinated seeds is that they are genetically stable enough to save seeds from these plants and expect the same plant to come back true to type. For gardeners who wish to build up a sustainable seed-saving practice continuously, this makes them popular.

15.2 Choosing Reputable Seed Sources

Gardening with quality seeds is highly recommended, and they come with great quality from reputed suppliers. Most seed catalogues from well-known companies will contain descriptions of germination rates, planting instructions for each variety, and any unique characteristics. High-quality heirloom seeds with excellent germination rates are well-known for Companies such as Baker Creek Heirloom Seed Co. and MI Gardener. However, local nurseries and garden centres are also valuable resources, as these also have local adaptation specialities.

Another great way to get high-quality seeds is to exchange and swap seeds with other gardeners. Such events enable you to exchange seeds and learn about plant varieties from various knowledge providers. Online heirloom seed companies, like Hudson Valley Seed Co. and Botanical Interests, have a variety of unique and rare seeds available, with very useful cultivation history and growing information on disc. Choose companies that are improving and contributing to the gardening community and seed sources, focusing on sustainable practices.

15.3 Evaluating Seed Packets

It is important to know how to read a seed packet. The variety name, Latin name, and whether or not the seeds are organic will be on the front of the packet. On the back of the packet, there is quite a bit of information about the variety, such as germination time, day to maturity, thinning recommendations, pest management (if applicable), and support structures.

For example, germination rate percentages indicate what percentage of seeds would germinate ideally. A higher germination rate, therefore, represents a better chance of a successful crop. It tells you how far apart to space out the soil to avoid overcrowding your plant, starting with planting depth instructions. Days to maturity will tell you how long it takes your plant to produce harvestable fruits or flowers so that you can plan your garden, plantings, etc., for continuous harvests. Not all seeds need special planting instructions such as pre-soaking or stratification (exposure to cold conditions), but this can greatly increase the likelihood of germination for certain types of seeds.

15.4 Factors Influencing Seed Quality

Several factors, such as potential storage conditions, age, and handling practices, all influence seed quality. Storage of seed is crucial to seed viability. Seeds should be stored in a cool, dry, dark place to avoid damage from heat or moisture. According to statistics, the storage temperature should be between 35 and 40°F, and relative humidity lower than 40%. For all practical purposes, seed storage in refrigerators is also used, but bringing the seeds to sealed containers to be protected from moisture is the most important.

Seed viability decreases over time, and having a single day to reseed is important as you learn the expiration dates on the seed packets. Some seeds, such as beans, squash, etc., may have long-living seeds for years, but there are seeds like onions and carrots, which only last one to two years. Handling the seeds gently is also important. Otherwise, rough handling can damage the mechanical process and decrease germination rates and seedling vigour. Poor quality signs in the seeds involve discolouration, mould, or a musty smell.

Interactive Element: Seed Packet Reading Exercise

Examine a few seed packets you have in your collection. Read the variety name, germination rate, planting depth, spacing, and days to maturity, as well as any special instructions. Record this information in a gardening journal or spreadsheet to plan your planting schedule and determine which varieties perform best.

Your garden begins with carefully putting your money towards selecting high-quality seeds, followed by reading what information is on the back of your seed packet. This focus on details means that you are achieving a healthy start on your plants, maximizing the highest possibility of healthy, productive crops.

15.5 Saving Seeds for Future Harvests

Saving seeds involves more than just the practical tasks of caring for the seeds and planting them again the next year; it is a way to connect to your garden on a deeper level. This is a major advantage because it saves money. Saving seeds from your best plants also puts you on the path of only having to buy new seeds once a year to have them for the following growing season — obviously, there is a ton of money you will ultimately save by doing this. By investing those savings into other parts of your homestead, this practice allows you to do so. Moreover, saving seeds also helps maintain special or rare plant varieties. Biodiversity in commercial agriculture is often sacrificed for a strict range of products, but in your garden, it is an act of preservation.

The next advantage of seed saving is that it helps cultivate plant adaptation to local climate and soil. So, over generations, seeds you save from plants adapted to your conditions will be more robust and a good match for your home. This adaptation results in more potent, more productive plants that can withstand local pests and diseases. Additionally, saving seeds can help alleviate your garden's genetic diversity. Choose to grow multiple varieties of plants rather than one to take advantage of your garden ecosystem's increased resilience and health.

Select healthy, vigorous plants with appealing features when deciding on seed-saving plants. The first step is to select disease-free plants as it is more likely that the offspring of this will be strong. Search for plants with high yields and strong growth, as they will help in future harvests. Also, pay some attention to the flavour and the size, for example, vegetables and fruits. For example, a seed-saving candidate is a tomato plant that produces large, tasty fruits. If you'd like true-to-type seeds, avoid saving them off hybrid plants. The hybrids may not produce offspring with desirable traits when mated.

Saving seeds from different plant types requires specific methods. For tomatoes, start by choosing fully ripe fruits. Cut them open and scoop out the seeds along with the surrounding gel. Place the seeds and gel in a jar with water and let it sit for a few days. This fermentation process helps remove the gel coating, which can inhibit germination. After a few days, rinse the seeds thoroughly and spread them out to dry on a paper towel.

Lettuce seeds are relatively easy to save. Allow one or two plants to bolt and produce flowers. Once the flowers have dried and formed seed heads, gently strip the seeds into a bowl. Separate the seeds from the chaff by lightly blowing on them or using a sieve. Basil seeds can be saved by allowing the plant to flower and produce seed heads. Once the seed heads are dry, rub them between your hands to dislodge the seeds. For marigolds, wait until the flower heads are completely dry. Remove the petals and gently shake the seeds free.

Proper seed storage and labelling are crucial for maintaining seed viability. Use airtight containers or envelopes to store your seeds, as exposure to air and moisture can reduce their longevity. Label each container with the plant variety and date of collection to keep track of your seeds and ensure you use the oldest seeds first. Store your seeds in a superb, dry, dark location, such as a basement or a refrigerator. Periodically test stored seeds for germination by placing a few seeds on a damp paper towel in a sealed bag. After a few days, check how many seeds have sprouted to gauge their viability.

Interactive Element: Seed Saving Journal

Start a seed-saving journal to document your efforts. Record the plant varieties, dates of seed collection, and any observations about the plants' performance. Note which plants produced the best seeds and any adjustments you made to your seed-saving techniques. This journal will become an invaluable resource for improving your seed-saving practices and ensuring a successful garden year after year.

You can create a sustainable seed bank for your garden by following these steps to save and store seeds. This practice not only saves you money but also allows you to cultivate plants that are uniquely adapted to your local conditions. Seed saving connects you to the cycles of growth and renewal in your garden, fostering a deeper appreciation for the plants you nurture. As you refine your seed-saving skills, you'll find yourself more attuned to the needs of your garden and better equipped to support its thriving ecosystem.

CHAPTER 16 DIY PROJECTS
FOR SELF-SUFFICIENCY

The very day, I cut the first piece of tree stump and decided to build my first compost bin. I had just pruned my tomato plants and made lots of trimmings. I stared at the pile and considered what it was worth. Even horrid, tidied-up packages should end up elsewhere in the garbage. At that point, I started to compost. This was a game changer for my garden, as well as for how I approach waste and how I live sustainably.

16.1 Building a Compost Bin

Making a compost bin is among the most important projects in your backyard. Kitchen and garden waste is reduced, and compost is generated for good soil-enriching compost. The ability to increase your nutrient levels, therefore, will decrease the need for you to rely on artificial store-bought fertilizers, favouring sustainable gardening. This is nature's way of recycling – making black gold of your plants that otherwise would turn into waste.

First, talking about how to reduce waste. Scraps of vegetables, coffee grounds, and eggshells are all produced in every kitchen, but they often get thrown away. Composting these sends much of your household waste to landfills for it. Garden waste, such as leaves, grass clippings, and small branches, are the same. Composting turns these materials into valuable organic matter instead of burning or discharging them. This also creates less waste and lessens your carbon footprint and methane emissions since it produces less organic waste in landfills.

The compost made from these scraps is the nutrient bounty for any gardener. Compost helps improve soil structure, retain moisture, and increase essential plant nutrients. A natural fertilizer, it cuts down on the need for chemical substitutes. Thus, when you include compost in your garden, you get a healthier, more productive one. This practice perfectly aligns with sustainable gardening, creating a closed loop where waste can become part of the resource.

While picking materials for your compost bin, you want something durable and cheaper. Recycled pallets are an eco-friendly option. Often free or cheap, they are easily available at local businesses or on online marketplaces. Compost bins can be built using sturdy pallets to create a simple yet effective design. Treated wood is a more polished option, though some gardeners prefer untreated wood to avoid leaching chemicals. Metal bins tend to be more durable, but they can be more expensive and may require some welding skills. Consequently, plastic containers are easy to care for and come in different sizes. Small spaces require small appliances, and these are just in perfect form!

Now, we move on to building your compost bin. For a pallet compost bin, acquire the necessary material first: four to six pallets, screws or nails, and a drill or hammer. Start with standing upright two pallets to serve as sides and secure them with screws or nails. Add two more pallets as front and back to make the box. You can also connect a fifth pallet as the bottom for added stability. Use any extra pallets to make a lid that will enable you to keep the heat and moisture in. Such a structure offers enough air to do the composting process.

A wooden compost bin will require untreated or treated lumber, a saw, screws, and a drill. Cut some wood to your required dimensions (a normal size is 3x3x3 feet). Put the side sections onto the corner posts, then clamp and attach the front and back panels. Space the slats so there is a little room for ventilation. Materials will be added quickly with a hinged lid, and the compost will turn. If you are looking for a sturdy and customizable bin, this type of bin is what you want.

If you want a compost bin made of wire mesh, first gather chicken wire or hardware cloth, metal stakes, and zip ties or wire. You can cut the wire to the desired height and length and mould it into a cylinder or square. Zip-tie the ends, then drive metal stakes while anchoring the enclosure to the ground. It is an excellent airflow design and can easily be moved if needed. This is for someone who needs a quick and low-cost option.

Compost bin maintenance is key to producing compost of good quality. The better aeration that results from turning the compost regularly speeds up decomposition. Mix the pile weekly or two with a pitchfork or compost aerator. To break down optimally, greens (nitrogen-rich material such as vegetable scraps and grass clippings) should be balanced with browns (carbon-rich material such as leaves and cardboard). Look for a 2 to 3 parts brown to 1 part green ratio. Secondly, moisture needs to be monitored, and the compost should be as damp as a wrung-out sponge. Add water or more greens if it hasn't turned out too dry. If you are too wet, add more browns and turn the pile to assist in aeration.

It's ready to use when your compost is dark, crumbly, and has an earthy smell. Harvest the finished compost by sifting it through a screen to separate any large, undecomposed pieces. These can be returned to the bin for further breakdown. Apply the compost to your garden by mixing it into the soil or as a top dressing. The nutrient boost will benefit your plants, leading to healthier growth and bountiful harvests.

Interactive Element: Compost Bin Maintenance Checklist

- **Turn the Compost Regularly:** Use a pitchfork or compost aerator to mix the pile every week or two.
- **Balance Greens and Browns:** Aim for a ratio of about 2-3 parts browns to 1 part greens.
- **Monitor Moisture Levels:** Ensure the compost is as damp as a wrung-out sponge. Add water or more greens if too dry; add more browns if too wet.
- **Harvesting Finished Compost:** Sift the compost to separate large pieces. Mix the finished compost into the soil or use it as a top dressing.

Building and maintaining a compost bin is a great positive activity regarding self-sufficiency. Kitchens and gardens provide value from recycling: compost valuable soil amendment. Composting is a simple task that benefits you greatly in many ways, turning your waste into a valuable ingredient in your garden, whether you choose pallets, wood, metal, or plastic for your bin.

16.2 DIY Cold Frames and Cloche Systems

As seasons change, extending or protecting your growing season and protecting your plants from adverse weather conditions can be a game changer. Two simple yet effective solutions to this would be cold frames and cloches. A cold frame is a small greenhouse that captures solar heat and has a microclimate extending into the fall and early spring growing seasons. Young plants are shielded from frost, wind, heavy rain, and even early snow or freeze that would interfere with their getting a head start on the growing season. Hardening off seedlings before transplanting them to the garden gives the seedlings a better chance of thriving outdoors.

The cold frame materials you use are important to select. Old windows make an excellent frame lid. This allows maximum sun on your plants and, in turn, gives insulation. Wooden planks may be a dependable choice for the structure. They are sustainable, easy to work with, and sturdy. If you are budgeting, polyethene sheeting is a good alternative for the lid. Lightweight, cheap, and still does a decent job of trapping heat. Adjustable hinges will make your cold frame more functional. They allow the frame to be opened for ventilation, saving your plants from becoming overheated during sunny days.

Building a cold frame is something that can be done relatively easily. Begin with making the wooden frame. Measure and cut your wooden planks along with them to the shape you want them up to 3 ft x 6 ft, and assemble them with screws or nails. Using the base will form your cold frame. Next, install the lid. Attach an old window with hinges to the frame if you use an old one.

Most importantly, this allows you to open or close the lid to ventilate your plants and maintain their protection. Polyethylene sheeting: staple it to the frame, and it should be tight so it doesn't sag. Bubbling up and around the inner sides of the cold frame insulates the cold frame by adding a straw or bubble wrap layer. This also helps retain heat on more freezing nights.

Cloches provide other protection for individual plants or small groups. With this tool, they will create a warm, sheltered environment around your plants that will protect them from frost, wind, and pests. Depending on your availability, you can make cloches from many materials. It is popular to use plastic bottles. This is pretty simple; removing the base of a large bottle and placing it over your plant will suffice. That is a mini greenhouse effect, trapping heat and moisture. Wire and plastic cloches are designed for use in larger plants. Cover chicken wire or hardware cloth in a cylinder with clear plastic. Zip ties or clips can securely secure the plastic to ensure it does not come loose. The actual cloche itself is a more aesthetic option than glass bell cloches, as they offer great protection and a hint of elegance.

Overheating has to be prevented by ventilating cloches. During sunny days, lift the cloche slightly or remove it completely to let air go through. The openings allow the heat and humidity to escape, which helps prevent them from building up. Ensure the temperature and moisture levels inside the cloche are comfortable, and check often. Hardening off seedlings is most important to cloches. As they strengthen, increase the time outdoors by removing the cloche for a few hours daily. Acclimatizing them this way allows them to adjust to the conditions the garden will put them into.

Building and using cold frames and cloches is a worthwhile use of time if you invest it since they extend your growing season and protect your plants from unpredictable weather. Your garden thus gets favourable microclimates that support robust growth and early harvests with these structures. Building cold frames using recycled windows or cloches from plastic bottles is practical and rewarding, so these projects hop from the yard work bucket into the Self-sufficient backyard.

CHAPTER 17 PRESERVING YOUR HARVEST

One sunny afternoon, I had a universe of tomatoes, enough cucumbers to meet my monthly needs, and enough peaches to serve as material for toasting breadcrumbs. As a homesteader, no one harvests more than they do. What pleases me more is when my entire garden holds a full harvest. However, it wasn't long before I knew that I couldn't keep all this abundance until it was cold again. It was then that I learned how to can and jar — a method of prolonging the life of your produce and reliving the summer flavour year round. So here's a basic guide to canning and jarring for beginners to get you through the growing season and enjoy your harvest months past.

17.1 Canning and Jarring for Beginners

Time-tested methods for preserving food and, when stored, fruits, vegetables, and even meats without refrigeration—canning and jarring. Sealing food in sterilized jars and processing it in the vacuum you create, playing the role of a boil water bath or a pressure canner prevents the food from spoiling. This is a process that maintains food that is nutritious and tasty while keeping it safe.

That is why one of the most crucial steps in canning is sterilizing your jars and lids. Sterilization will prevent any harmful bacteria or mould from contaminating the pre-served food. Wash them in hot, soapy water until the jars, lids, and bands are clean. Place the jars in a large pot of boiling water and keep them there for at least 10 minutes. Keep the jars in the hot water until you are ready to fill them. Boilable lids and bands should not be boiled; putting lids and bands in a simmering pot of water is okay.

Knowing how acidity plays a role in food preservation is important in picking the ideal canned food method. Fruits, jams, pickles, and other high-acid foods have a pH of 4.6 or below and inhibit the growth of harmful bacteria. And they can be safely processed using the water bath canning method. Pressure canning is used to bring vegetables, meats, and soups, all of which are low-acid foods, up to high enough temperatures to kill a risk of botulism. This serious disease is caused by bacteria that thrive in low-acid, low-oxygen environments.

Water bath canning will require a canner or a large pot with a wire rack, jars (Mason or Kilner), and canning lids (two parts). They also include pH strips, funnels, bubble removers, magnetic lid wands, and timers (all optional). Preserving high-acid foods is possible by using water bath canning. It ensures that the food stays safe and delicious for months.

Start by sanitizing and sterilizing your canning jars and lids. Put the prepared food into the jars and leave enough headspace, usually about half an inch to an inch, depending on the recipe. It gives food expansion space in the process. Run a nonmetallic utensil inside the edge of the jar to re-move any air bubbles. Rinse the rims clean with a damp cloth to ensure a good seal; place the lids on top and screw the bands on tight enough to leave an impression from your knuckles.

Secondly, submerge the filled jars into the canner in at least one inch of water. Process the jars for the time stated in your recipe and for the duration of time specified for your recipe if it requires processing at a higher altitude. After the processing time, put the heat off, leave the jars in the water for a couple of minutes, and remove them. Once jars are filled, you carefully lift jars out with canning tongs and put them on a clean towel to cool undisturbed for 2 to four days. Press down on the centre of each lid and check the seals. The jar is sealed if it doesn't pop back. Storing your jars in a cool, dark place for up to a year is a good idea to label and store them.

However, pressure connoting is essential for preserving low-acid foods. To be able to use a pressure canner, you'll need one; it is a pressure cooker that is astoundingly different from a pressure cooker; that is, its sole purpose is providing canners for food. Start by assembling and inspecting your pressure canner according to the manufacturer's directions. Ensure the seals are intact and the vent pipe is clear of obstructions.

Fill your jars with low-acid foods like green beans or chicken soup, and add the recommended amount of liquid (water or broth). The correct headspace is left, and the air bubbles are removed. After wiping clean rims, put on lids and secure them with bands on top.

According to the manufacturer, place the jars into the pressure canner and add several inches of water. Bring the canner to a boil and lock the lid in place. The steam should vent for 10 minutes before placing the weight or pressure regulator on the vent pipe. Place the canner on the stove, heat it for the time specified in your recipe, and let it come to the right pressure—10 to 15 pounds, depending on altitude—and process the jars.

When processing is finished, turn off the heat and allow the canner to cool down naturally. It can take an hour or several more. Please do not attempt to quicken the cooling process because it can crack the jars or spoil the food. Wait until the canner depressurizes. Gently remove the lid and lift out the jars with canning tongs. Cool the jars for 24 hours by placing them on a towel and checking them for seals as previously described.

Easy recipes for beginners going off to a fresh start will give you the confidence needed and help you succeed. A classic for strawberry jam is strawberries, sugar, and lemon juice. Cucumbers pickled with vinegar, water, salt, and spices are another favourite. Apple butter, made of apple, sugar, and spices, is a spread well suited to toast, and tomato sauce is one of the most versatile things, usable in many dishes.

Canning and jarring is not such a mystery; by learning the basics and mastering the art of preserving your harvest, you can enjoy the fruits of your labour all year round. These techniques are for those new to homesteading as well as those experienced in the art of backyard gardening.

17.2 Freezing and Drying Techniques

During harvest season, your garden can yield more produce than those that can fresh. Freezing and drying help in that case. The preservation methods do not only seem simple but practical as well. They freeze-lock in nutrients and flavour so you can enjoy the summer harvests all winter. However, drying reduces the size and weight of your product for storage. These techniques lengthen your fruit and vegetable's shelf life from additive-free, and your pantry will be stocked with the nutritious, grown-at-home food you crave.

One of the quickest ways to preserve your fresh produce is freezing. Since it can be so effective on fruits and vegetables that you intend to cook, this is the ideal steamer for food. First, start blanching your vegetables to ensure they are high quality and have no freezer burn. A brief boiling of the vegetables and plunging into ice water is involved in this process. Blanching kills bacteria, stops enzymes from going into action, prevents degradation of the quality of the food, and helps retain vitamins and minerals. For instance, blanch asparagus for 2-3 minutes and immediately cool in ice water; pat dry thoroughly.

Patting vegetables is then followed by proper packaging. Place quart-, gallon- or vacuum-sealed freezer bags to avoid flavour and freezer burn. Make sure there's as little air that can be removed when packing. Before freezing, spread fruits and vegetables in a single layer on a baking sheet so they will not clump. Transfer them after they're frozen solid to your storage bags. Organize and label your frozen produce; don't forget. Each bag should be written with the date and contents so you can track what you have. To maintain the flavour and texture when you use your frozen produce, thaw it slowly in the refrigerator.

Another excellent way to preserve your harvest is to dry fruits and vegetables. This method removes the moisture from the food, preventing the growth of bacteria, yeast, and mould. But all types can be dried with air, an oven, or, most commonly, a food dehydrator. Different methods have their benefits depending on what type of produce is being washed.

Air drying is a traditional method best suited for herbs and leafy greens. Bunch together small amounts of herbs like basil, thyme, or rosemary, tie these together and then hang them upside down in a dry area. When they are leafy greens such as kale and spinach, you can spread them out on a clean screen or rack. They should be shaded to prevent the leaves from turning bitter.

Fruits and vegetables are easy to dry in the oven. The oven is preheated as low as possible, usually at 140 F. Slice fruits like apples and peaches into uniform pieces for even drying. Line the baking sheets with parchment paper and place them. The oven should be left with the door slightly ajar to escape moisture. Turn the pieces to check the produce so it dries as evenly as possible. Patience is the key because this method can take several hours.

When your produce has been dried, it is now important to store it properly to prevent the quality from going down. For moisture and airproofing, airtight containers or vacuum-sealed bags are used. Place the containers in a pantry or cupboard, and store the containers in a cool, dark, dry place. Check frequently for moisture, spoilage like mould, or bad smell. Discard the affected product if you find any issues. To prepare, you use dried fruits and vegetables in cooking; you can rehydrate them by soaking them in water or broth until they become plump.

It's like suddenly opening a world of culinary possibilities for drying produce. Healthy snacks and easy preparation are offered by drying apple slices. Slice the apples thinly, dunk them in lemon juice to stop browning, and dry them till leathery but still pliable. Sun drying adds flavour to salads, pasta dishes, and sandwiches. Ripe tomatoes, slice, salt, and dry them until chewy and intense. Store-bought snacks like beet and kale chips are a good source of dehydrated vegetable chips. To add a sweet treat, puree a little fruit, spread it thinly onto a dehydrator tray or baking pan, and dry it until it's flexible but not tacky.

Freezing and drying will extend the life of your garden's bounty, and you can enjoy it during the year by incorporating these techniques. These methods are easy to use and are perfect for harvesting the maximum harvest from their yields.

CHAPTER 18 BUDGET-FRIENDLY HOMESTEADING

On a chilly morning, I was watching the price tags in a local store of garden supplies, and it felt dizzying. With a limited budget, I planned to have a grand back patio. At that point, I got creative. I could innovate how to turn everyday household items into valuable gardening tools, stretch my dollars far, and still have a thriving garden. The central purpose of this chapter is to support those who would like to create a beautiful or productive garden without having the bank to burn.

18.1 Thrifty Gardening Tips

Household items can be repurposed to change the game regarding gardening on a budget. One of the simplest savings to boost your garden would be to use egg cartons as seed starters. Cardboard or styrofoam containers are great for beginning seeds. Put the seeds in each compartment, the soil, and the carton outside in the sun. When the seedlings are ready for transplanting, you can cut the compartments apart and directly transplant them into the soil, as the cardboard will decompose independently.

Mini cloches can also be created from plastic bottles and paper bags, protecting young seedlings from frost and pests. Use old plastic bottles to cut the bottoms off and put them over your seedling to make a tiny greenhouse effect. In addition, this is how money is saved and helps recycle plastic waste. Also, you can make plant markers with popsicle sticks or old cutlery. All you have to do is write the plant name on the stick or the handle and plant it next to your plants in the soil. As simple and creative an idea as this is to keep track of what you've planted, it is.

Another great idea is to use old bed frames or ladders to make them garden trellises. These items can be obtained free or at a reduced cost at local recycling centres or through Freecycle networks. An old metal bed frame can be fashioned as a sturdy trellis for climbing plants such as beans and cucumbers. Wooden ladders are great supports for vining plants because they secure such plants very well when leaned against a fence or wall. Repurposing these items will save money and bring a nice twist of fresh style to your garden.

It doesn't need to be a difficult task to find affordable gardening materials. First, visit a local recycling centre, Freecycle Networks, for free or cheap materials such as wood, metal, and containers. They have also devised the great idea of community plant swaps and seed exchanges. However, at these events, you can trade plants and seeds with other gardeners and grow more plants without spending money. Scavenging wood pallets and crates will also yield materials in raised beds, compost bins, and other garden structures. Check sites like Craigslist or Facebook Marketplace for free or cheap tools and supplies. The good thing about many people wishing to 'get rid' of items they no longer need is that you can often pick up gardening tools and other essentials at a fraction of the retail price.

Another way to save money is to start working on the DIY garden projects. Reclaimed wood building raised beds is a great example. Disassembled and reconfigured into sturdy raised beds, wood pallets (often free) can be used instead of metal ones. Ensure that the wood isn't treated already so that it does not contaminate your garden with chemicals. Another back-of-the-envelope price that further reduces the cost is to create a drip irrigation system using recycled materials. Water delivered to your plant's roots saves money and water, and old hoses, plastic tubing, and milk jugs can all be found in your recycle and reused for delivering water to your plant's roots.

Using old pallets to construct a compost bin is quite practical and economical. And for those of us with limited growing space, with a little effort, you can assemble a simple three-sided structure that leaves its front open so that we can quickly use compost kitchen scraps and yard waste, constantly adding nutrient-rich compost to our garden. Another fantastic rain barrel project is to make one out of a repurposed plastic drum. Installing a spigot that can attach the barrel to your gutter downspout will allow you to collect and store rainwater to water your garden instead of using municipal water.

One of the clever gardening techniques for maximizing garden productivity on a budget involves using clever gardening techniques to maximize your guests to your efforts. Rather than planting new crops immediately, moving into succession planting and planting your next crop immediately after harvesting the old will keep your garden productive from spring to fall. This method allows you to continue harvesting and having fresh produce. There is also the technique of companion planting. With a little strategy, you can couple two plants that help each other, work on pest control, and increase yields. An example is planting basil with tomatoes, as it would repel harmful insects and improve the flavour of the tomatoes.

It is very important to practice crop rotation to maintain soil fertility and avoid the buildup of pests and diseases. Every year, rotate your crops so that no plant family grows in the same place year after year. Balancing soil nutrients and disrupting pest cycles are the two advantages of this practice. Beans and zucchini are also growing crops that are high-yield and low-cost. These plants are easy to grow, don't require much investment, and have terrific yields. For example, beans can be sown into the soil and are liable to yield more than enough for your family members and give away to neighbours.

By incorporating these thrifty gardening tips, you can create a beautiful and productive garden without spending a fortune. Repurposing household items, sourcing affordable materials, and implementing clever gardening techniques will help you achieve your gardening goals while staying within your budget.

18.2 DIY Homemade Fertilizers and Pesticides

Commercial fertilizers and pesticides were expensive, so when I first started gardening, I quickly learned how. They also stressed my budget, and I worried about the chemicals I put into my garden. It was then I turned to homemade alternatives. The first cost is that it saves money when making fertilizers and pesticides. Repurposing kitchen and garden waste decreases the amount of waste landfilled and the amount of chemicals exposed to your plants and soil. Also, you can customize these solutions to your garden's exact needs.

The significant advantage of homemade fertilizers and pesticides is that they reduce the need for commercial products. Hefty price tags and synthetic chemicals often accompany most purchased commercial products. You can create your own, providing healthier soil and plants. Moreover, kitchen and garden waste is recycled sustainably when used, meaning the items usually thrown away are recycled by gardening.

Compost tea is one of my favourite homemade fertilizers. The one you have is an alcohol that has a nutrient: it's been steeping compost in water. To make it, put compost in a burlap sack or old pillowcase, submerge in a five-gallon bucket of water, and steep for about a week. Aerating the mixture, stir it daily. It's ready when it's ready, then dilute the tea with water in a 1:10 ratio and apply it to your plants. This tea will add health to your soil, making plant growth healthier.

An eggshell calcium amendment is an easy, effective fertilizer as well. Rinse your eggshells, dry your eggshells, and save your eggshells for this purpose. Eventually, dry them and grind them into a fine powder using a mortar, pestle, food processor, or something else. Dust around your plants for a calcium supply is necessary for making cell walls and general plant health. Preventing blossom end rot in tomatoes and peppers is particularly useful.

Potassium is also abundant in banana peels, which are excellent for flowering and fruiting. All you have to do is chop the peels of the fruits and flowers and bury them in the soil around your plants. You can also make banana peel tea by making peels in water for several days. Look at this tea as a plant fertilizer and boost the potassium in your plant. Another fantastic one is from the coffee grounds. Sprinkled directly into the soil or your compost pile, they are nitrogen-rich. Avoid using them too much, as too much nitrogen can sometimes injure the plants.

There are several practical and inexpensive homemade pesticides. The best type of spraying with garlic and chilli is against various pests. Puree a few cloves of garlic and hot peppers with some water to make it. Then, let the mixture sit overnight, strain it, and add a few drops of dish soap. This solution can be sprayed on your plants to keep away aphids, caterpillars, and the like. Another strong natural pesticide is neem oil. Both fungal issues and insects are countered well with it. In a gallon of water, dissolve a table-spoon of neem oil and a teaspoon of liquid soap and spray this on affected plants.

Simple soap and water sprays are very effective for soft-bodied insects such as aphids, spider mites, and white flies. Spray some mild dishwashing liquid and a quart of water onto the pests directly; a few drops out of every quart. This soap breaks down its outer layer and dehydrates and dies. Diatomaceous earth is a natural powder with fossilized al-gae mixed inside. When worn as a cloth, it is a mechanical insecticide sprinkled around the base of plants. The exo-skeletons of insects like slugs, ants, and beetles are cut through by the tiny sharp edges of the particles, dehydrat-ing them.

All these homemade solutions are crucial, and they will work only if they are applied correctly. Timing is every-thing. Fertilizers should be applied in the morning or late afternoon because the soil will absorb them this way, the evaporation is much less, and the nutrients are less. Pesti-cides should be sprayed late in the day because beneficial insects, such as bees and ladybugs, are less active. It de-creases the chance of harming these garden helpers.

Do not use any method to prevent any damage to your plants. So, for example, too much compost tea is likely to bring nutrient imbalances, and overuse of neem oil can burn plant leaves. You constantly watch over the health of your plants and change the treatment accordingly. Combined, multiple methods work particularly well, known as integrated pest management or IPM. You increase the resiliency of your garden ecosystem using various techniques to make your garden better to stand up against pests and diseases.

Both of these DIY fertilizers and pesticides can save you money and allow you to help rid your garden of unwanted visitors for a healthier, more sustainable garden. Customized care will help your plants thrive, and you will be satisfied knowing exactly what is in the food you are growing. The more you get used to creating and using these homemade solutions types, the more you'll discover they are a fantastic environmentally friendly bet against commercially sold products.

 ∾

CHAPTER 19 SUSTAINABLE PRACTICES AND PERMACULTURE

It all started one afternoon while wandering through a local community garden. I stumbled upon a plot that seemed to thrive effortlessly. The garden appeared to be a self-sustaining ecosystem, buzzing with life and productivity. Curious, I started conversing with the gardener, who introduced me to permaculture. This holistic approach to agriculture transformed my tiny backyard and reshaped my understanding of sustainable living.

19.1 Permaculture Principles for Small Spaces

Working with, rather than against, nature is a part of permaculture, a philosophy. Its idea is to make natural processes that create harmonious, self-sustaining ecosystems. Of all permaculture ethics, at its core, there are three: earth care, people care, and fair share. It is earth care and the importance of using the earth to be cared for in maintaining the health of the soil and supporting biodiversity. People's care is related to caring for oneself and the community, having regard for well-being and resilience. Fair sharing emphasizes the benefit of sharing surplus and redistributing resources to make them equitable.

Permaculture principles can have a specific effect on small-scale backyard farming. There are self-sustaining eco-systems that you can create that are as efficient as possible and produce as little waste as possible. Then, you can create a garden by observing natural patterns and interactions; the work it needs is minimal. In addition to reducing resource use and eliminating waste, nutrients are recycled into the system. But it's an approach for the environment and pro-duces a low-maintenance, productive garden.

Small-space gardening can only happen with permacul-ture design principles. The first steps comprise observation and interaction. Understand your garden's natural pattern, such as sunlight, wind, or water flow. Knowledge gained from this will let you create a garden complementary to its surroundings. Rainwater harvesting systems and solar pan-els can catch and store energy. These also save resources and fuel and help provide a sustainable energy supply to your garden. Growing food crops and possibly raising chickens are a means of obtaining a yield. To get something beneficial out of your efforts, be it vegetables, fruits, or Eggs. Polycultures and companion planting for use and values diversity. Plantings of diverse plants create ecosys-tems that require fewer pesticides and are less prone to pests and disease.

Organizing your garden into permaculture zones makes designing it much easier. Zone 0 is your home and your close surroundings. The kitchen garden area includes where you grow herbs and vegetables that you use often. Inten-sive-use areas of the garden are defined by Zone 1, which includes the vegetable gardens and herb beds. You visit these places daily, so put these places in your proximity. Semi-intensively managed areas such as fruit trees and chicken coops are included in Zone 2. Less frequent but still needing constant care, these areas need more attention. Compost heaps and woodlots are all considered in Zone 3, less frequently managed areas. These zones are farther from your home, and minimal maintenance is needed.

Permaculture techniques can be used for practical and rewarding small spaces. If space is not on your side, key-hole garden beds are an excellent way to use your space. These beds are easy to access for plants in excellent growing areas. The circular design has the composting basket in the centre, which means nutrients are readily available to your plants. Another technique that improves fertility and moisture retention is Hugelkultur beds. Logs, branches, and other organic materials are used as a base to create a very rich, decomposing environment that holds water and stimulates the growth of plants. Vertical gardens and trellises are the best for using your planting space in tiny spaces. Upwards-growing plants save space and circulate air, which reduces pest and disease problems. Windbreaks and features, including water, can create microclimates that increase your garden's productivity. Sheltered areas and the addition of objects such as ponds or birdbaths support beneficial insects and the balance of an ecosystem.

Interactive Element: Permaculture Design Exercise

Sketch your yard and determine the separate zones in your yard. Aside from these, note where you can get involved in rainwater harvesting, vertical gardens, and other keyhole beds. Think about ways you could companion plants with chickens or other small livestock and where you could integrate such animals. Therefore, this exercise will help you to imagine what your garden can look like and then make appropriate decisions when applying permaculture principles.

Permaculture truly brings your small backyard to a thriving, self-sustaining ecosystem. This gardening approach provides support for environmental health and helps to link with your community as well as nature. Because these principles don't have to be applied to large spaces, the rewards are plentiful, even in the smallest spaces.

19.2 Zero-Waste Gardening Practices

Zero-waste gardening means getting the most out of what you have and minimizing waste. This approach suits sustainability down to the ground, focusing on resource efficiency and reducing our environmental footprint on this planet. Turning garden and kitchen waste that would otherwise be thrown into the trash bin into compost is composting. It is a simple way of improving soil health and decreasing the usage of supplemental fertilizers. Closed loop life within your garden can be achieved by reducing dependence on single-use plastics, like reusable containers and biodegradable materials.

Preserving kitchen and garden waste by composting is a cornerstone of being a zero-waste gardener. Save kitchen scraps such as vegetables, coffee, and eggshells. These items are high in nitrogen and will speed up this process. The compost pile can add garden clippings, fallen leaves, and small branches. These materials supply the carbon to balance the kitchen waste containing excessive nitrogen. Compost bins or tumblers are used to contain compost and to make turning it easier. There are also worms in the vermicomposting—breaking down organic matter—which is highly effective for small spaces. Proper composting is all about how much green and brown materials are used. Desire a ratio of about 2 to 3 parts brown to 1 part green by keeping the compost damp as it can be wrung out of a sponge.

Natural mulches and ground covers reduce the amount of waste and are good for the garden's health. The straw, wood chips, and leaves used as mulch will help retain soil moisture, suppress weeds, and provide organic matter to the soil as it breaks down. Cover crops, like clover and vetch, are good to plant; they will help with nitrogen in the soil and prevent erosion. Living mulches also protect the soil and provide desirable habitat for beneficial insects. In small, intensively planted gardens, a thick piece of mulch helps reduce evaporation in the summer and keeps the soil warmer in the winter; it usually provides two benefits:

Upcycling garden materials will help reduce waste and give your space a character that cannot be found in other stores. Raised beds made of reclaimed wood are cheap and help prevent the wasted energy of transporting material. Stairy, attractive beds can be created by looking for old pallets or unused lumber. Old tools and containers can be turned into charming garden art by creating garden art from her. Sculpture or functional art pieces from old watering cans, shovels, and all those broken tools. It is practical and eco-friendly to re-cycle plant markers from broken pottery or old cutlery. Place these items in your garden and write the plant names on these items. Upcycling materials that would otherwise land in a landfill is another way to up-cycle; this time, it's using old tyres as planters or garden borders.

Integrating these zero-waste gardening practices into your routine contributes to a more sustainable and environmentally friendly garden. Composting, using natural mulches, and repurposing materials reduce waste and enhance your garden's health and productivity. These practices create a closed-loop system where resources are recycled and reused, minimizing the need for external inputs and reducing your environmental footprint. Embracing zero-waste gardening is a step towards a more self-sufficient and resilient homestead.

As you implement these practices, you'll find that your garden becomes more efficient and less reliant on external resources. The benefits extend beyond your garden, contributing to a more sustainable lifestyle. By reducing waste and using resources more efficiently, you create a healthier environment for yourself and future generations. This holistic approach to gardening aligns with the broader principles of sustainability and self-sufficiency, making it an integral part of modern backyard farming. The journey towards a zero-waste garden is rewarding and impactful, fostering a deeper connection to the earth and a more sustainable way of living.

In the next chapter, let's explore how these sustainable practices can be integrated into a complete permaculture system.

CHAPTER 20 COMMUNITY AND
CONTINUED LEARNING

I was conversing with another gardener at the local farmers market on a Saturday afternoon, and we discussed the proper approach for battling tomato blight. While swapping tips and listening to each other's stories, I realised how important these community connections were. Even so, gardening is a very social activity: growing in a community. Local gardening clubs and community projects will turn your backyard farming experience into wisdom, support, and camaraderie.

20.1 Local Resources and Gardening Clubs

This could provide many benefits in connection with local gardening communities and resources. First, you are given practical, region-specific advice you would not find in a generic gardening book. Since the local gardeners know your climate, soil, and what can be expected regarding pests, their advice is invaluable. They know the tricks of your area and can provide what you are looking for in your gardening trials. Besides, it creates a camaraderie and a sense of mutual support while sharing their experiences and learning from other people. Knowing you're not alone in your gardening journey and that other people have experienced and surmounted the same problems is very comforting.

The second advantage is that it has access to local resources and support. Soil testing, workshops, manipulation of soils, and expert advice are free or low cost, and extension services and agricultural offices are available in many communities. When it comes to fresh produce, seedlings, and gardening supplies, local farmers' markets are too much of a wonderful way to find those, often at better prices than a commercial store. In addition, they allow you to get to know the local farmers and vendors, and you can learn a lot from them. Connect or build a network of like-minded people, and you can break bigger seeds with them, exchange seeds, share and use tools, or do some collaborative projects.

It's easier than you think to find local gardening clubs or groups. Firstly, you can find online community gardening groups in the area where you live. The Royal Horticultural Society (RHS) provides maps and directories from where you can find nearby groups. All local nurseries and garden centres have bulletin boards with information on local clubs and when events will be held. The library, community centre, coffee shop, and community bulletin boards are good places to check for leads. If you don't know someone, there's no harm in asking your neighbours and friends for recommendations of material or personnel you could use.

Community partnerships by engaging in community gardening projects come with many benefits. Gardening in a community garden allows you to use and learn from the shared resources and tools, and just by volunteering there, you gain access to the knowledge of more experienced gardeners. Please participate in neighbourhood garden initiatives, which often beautify public spaces and build green, productive areas for all of us. Participation in local garden tours and workshops, where gardening styles and techniques are revealed, inspires and nurtures practical knowledge. By teaming up for urban farming projects, we launch underutilized spaces such as beautiful gardens that contribute to food security and the beautification of the community.

Using available local resources is a territory where you can enhance your lumbering, planting, and processing efforts. Free or low-cost workshops, soil testing, and expert advice directed to your agricultural region are often provided at extension services and agricultural offices. The services are important in solving particular gardening problems and enhancing success in general. The farmer's market is not just for buying produce but also is a wonderful place to purchase your seedlings and gardening supplies and to meet local farmers and vendors. These professionals can be good sources of continuing support and access to locally adapted plants that can build relationships with these professionals.

Other great resources are the Cooperative Extension Master Gardener programs. These programs teach gardening education and support to the community through volunteering. They can personally advise master gardeners, offer workshops, or even visit a garden to diagnose a problem and offer a solution. They are a goldmine of information and can prove very helpful in terms of improving your gardening skills. The many botanical gardens and arboretums also have a variety of workshops and classes on different subjects like basic care, plant care, grafting, and even permaculture. The benefits of these educational opportunities are huge because they help you learn and perfect your gardening practices.

Interactive Element: Community Gardening Checklist

1. **Search Online:** Look for community gardening groups on websites and social media.
2. **Visit Local Nurseries:** Check bulletin boards for information about local clubs and events.
3. **Check Community Bulletin Boards:** Libraries, community centres, and coffee shops often post gardening events and groups.
4. **Ask Neighbors and Friends:** Personal recommendations can lead to valuable connections.
5. **Volunteer at Community Gardens:** Gain hands-on experience and meet fellow gardeners.
6. **Join Neighborhood Initiatives:** Participate in projects beautifying and greening your local area.
7. **Attend Garden Tours and Workshops:** Learn from experienced gardeners and get inspired by different gardening styles.
8. **Utilize Extension Services:** Use free or low-cost workshops, soil testing, and expert advice.
9. **Visit Farmers' Markets:** Network with local farmers and vendors to find high-quality seedlings and supplies.
10. **Engage with Master Gardener Programs:** Attend workshops, seek personalized advice, and enhance your gardening skills.

Integration into your local gardening community allows you to tap into a knowledge store, resource service, and support. This network makes you a better gardener and fills you with belonging and connection to your community. Joining in some way with a local gardening group or resource is something you can do, whether you're inquiring, sharing, or wanting to be part of something bigger.

20.2 Online Forums and Further Learning Opportunities

Today, online gardening communities have become a great tool for backyard farmers. Another benefit of belonging to these communities is interacting with a wide network of gardeners worldwide. You may be asking a question or working on a particular issue, and you can get immediate answers. Seasoned gardeners have wandered into these forums and done your battle for you many times. Instant access to expert advice can save you time and avoid potential mistakes.

Secondly, the fact that you can share your successes and share your mistakes in the global online gardening communities is another advantage. Putting a picture of your first ripe tomato or discussing the pests running amok in your garden can be a connection and support. Other peoples' triumphs and lessons from their setbacks are encouraging. In addition, these platforms are houses of new gardening trends, ideas, and techniques. This will provide you with ideas on implementing the latest innovative hydroponic setups and the latest in organic pest control to add to your garden.

It's easy to find forums and groups to join. First, check forums about gardening on popular sites like Reddit and GardenWeb. There are discussions about any vegetables to the ornamental plants on these platforms. There are also a number of groups on Facebook that are focused on backyard farming and homesteading. Look for terms like "backyard farming" and "urban homesteading" if you have a particular niche, e.g., hydroponics, permaculture, etc. Specific forums, such as Permies or Tomatoville, focus on the subject and provide support with discussions and resources. Because there are lots of hashtags for gardening, you can use Instagram and Twitter to follow them to get a nonstop stream of inspiration and gardening tips.

Gardening knowledge and skills can tremendously improve using materials available on the Internet. There are many online courses and webinars on various topics, from beginner gardening basics to more advanced grafting and soil health. An example is the "Let's Talk Gardens" webinar series offered on the Smithsonian Gardens channel. Another way of learning is through watching tutorial videos on YouTube channels. MIGardener and Epic Gardening are two sites that provide step-by-step guides and helpful tips for gardening. Looking up gardening blogs and eBooks also gives in-depth information about gardening from someone who has experienced it himself.

It's important to perpetually keep abreast of things you didn't even know you would want later. Gardening newsletters and magazines make you subscribe to them not for any particular reason but because they will give you regular updates on the new gardening methods developed for various plants. Social media keeps you updated on the advances of the gardening world by following gardening influencers and experts. Today, out of many influencers, plenty of them post daily hints, projects, or seasonal information. You can also learn from the leading experts by attending virtual gardening conferences or events and contacting other gardening enthusiasts. The presentations usually speak about the latest and upcoming practices and trends. The experience of online discussions and Q&A sessions allows you to ask questions, exchange your experiences, and learn from real-time inputs.

While joining online gardening communities might not guarantee knowledge, it brings you to a supportive community. It's quite motivating to have camaraderie and a shared love of gardening. These communities provide a wealth of resources and support for novice or veteran gardeners or homesteaders. Being part of the gardening community has benefits; you improve your gardening skills and share your collective gardening knowledge with the community. It feels good to know you belong and will help with mutual support during your gardening experience.

As such, let us dive into the online garden communities. Try online learning resources like forums, social media groups, etc. Continue to seed curiosity, be connected, and grow.

Conclusion

As we end our journey into backyard farming, let's take a moment to reflect on all that we've covered. This book started with the idea that you can create a thriving, self-sufficient homestead even with less than an acre of land. We've explored modern techniques, from outdoor gardening and greenhouses to hydroponics and water management. We've delved into the essentials of plant nutrients, learned the best planting and harvest times for various vegetables, and discussed crop proportions and sizing. We also touched on the importance of selecting and saving seeds. And let's not forget the chapters on raising chickens, which offer a rewarding addition to any backyard farm.

Throughout the book, you've discovered how to assess and improve soil quality, build and maintain raised beds, and maximize small spaces through container and vertical gardening. We've also covered efficient water management techniques, seasonal planting and crop rotation for soil health, and the importance of plant nutrients and soil amendments.

One of the key takeaways is that planning and organization are crucial. By understanding your space, budget, and time, you can make informed decisions that lead to a productive and sustainable backyard farm. The importance of composting and soil health can't be overstated, as they are the foundation of any successful garden. Raised beds and container gardening offer flexibility and efficiency, making them perfect for small spaces. Vertical gardening allows you to maximize your growing area, while efficient water management ensures your plants get the hydration they need without wasting resources.

Seasonal planting and crop rotation help maintain soil health and improve yields while understanding plant nutrients and using proper soil amendments to ensure plants have everything they need to thrive. Organic pest control methods and companion planting can naturally ward off pests and improve plant health. Growing vegetables, herbs, and spices add fresh, flavorful ingredients to your kitchen, and raising chickens provides fresh eggs and natural pest control.

Now, it's time to take action. Start by assessing your backyard and planning your homestead layout. Gather the materials you need, and begin with small, manageable projects. Whether building a raised bed, setting up a compost bin, or planting your first crops, every step brings you closer to a self-sufficient lifestyle. Don't be afraid to experiment and learn from your experiences. Gardening is as much about the journey as it is about the destination.

I want to express my deepest gratitude to you for embarking on this journey with me. Your dedication and enthusiasm for creating a self-sufficient homestead are genuinely inspiring. I hope this book has equipped you with the knowledge and confidence to transform your backyard into a productive and sustainable paradise. Remember, every garden is unique, and what works for one may not work for another. Be patient, stay curious, and enjoy learning and growing.

In closing, I leave you with this final thought: The beauty of backyard farming lies in its ability to bring us closer to nature and each other. It teaches us patience, resilience, and the value of hard work. It connects us to the earth and to the food we eat. Most importantly, it reminds us that even in the smallest of spaces, we have the power to create something beautiful and bountiful.

So, roll up your sleeves, dig into the soil, and let your backyard flourish. The journey to self-sufficiency is rewarding and filled with growth, learning, and endless possibilities. **Happy farming**!

References

- 7 Reasons to Create a Self-Sufficient Garden This Spring https://greencitizen.com/blog/7-reasons-for-creating-your-own-self-sufficient-garden-this-spring/#:~:text=Unlike%20traditional%20farming%2C%20a%20self,the%20conventional%20way%20of%20farming.

- An Amazing and Prolific Urban Homestead https://www.motherearthnews.com/homesteading-and-livestock/urban-homestead-zmaz09fmzraw/

- Building a Sustainable Farm in Your Backyard https://www.thecuttingedgelandscape.com/building-a-sustainable-farm-in-your-backyard-a-comprehensive-guide/

- 11 Tips for Homesteading on a Budget https://homesteadersofamerica.com/homesteading-on-a-budget/

- How to Test Your Garden Soil (And 3 DIY Tests) https://www.almanac.com/content/3-simple-diy-soil-tests

- 9 Organic Soil Amendments for Growing Vegetables https://www.tenthacrefarm.com/organic-soil-amendments-vegetables/

- How to Improve Your Soil's Structure, Feed ... https://www.lyngsogarden.com/community-resources/how-to-improve-your-soil-structure/

- Backyard Composting in 6 Steps https://cswd.net/composting/backyard-composting/

- Choosing the Best Materials for Raised Garden Beds: https://homesteadandchill.com/materials-raised-garden-beds/
- How to Build a Raised Garden Bed: Step-by-Step Guide https://homesteadandchill.com/how-to-build-raised-garden-bed/
- What Type of Garden Soil Is Best for Raised Beds? https://www.gardenary.com/blog/what-type-of-garden-soil-is-best-for-raised-beds
- 25 Container Garden Ideas to Enhance Your Outdoor Space https://www.marthastewart.com/1145807/creative-container-garden-ideas
- 10 Benefits of Vertical Gardening https://www.planetnatural.com/10-benefits-of-vertical-gardening/
- 20 Best Climbing Plants for Any Trellis, Pergola, or Fence https://www.thespruce.com/climbing-plants-for-trellis-8584701
- 35 Trellis Ideas for a Stunning, Supported Garden https://www.thespruce.com/garden-trellis-ideas-7370795
- Living walls: a way to a greener urban landscape https://ecobnb.com/blog/2021/10/living-walls-greener-urban-landscape/
- Step Drip Irrigation System Installation Guide https://school.sprinklerwarehouse.com/design-install/step-by-step-drip-irrigation-system-installation-guide/

- Rainwater Collection on the Homestead https://homesteadingfamily.com/rainwater-collection-on-the-homestead/
- Safe Use of Household Greywater | New Mexico State University https://pubs.nmsu.edu/_m/M106/
- The 9 Best Rain Barrels of 2024, Tested and Reviewed https://www.thespruce.com/best-rain-barrels-6743830
- 2024 First and Last Frost Dates https://www.almanac.com/gardening/frostdates
- How to Grow Early Spring Vegetables - Longwood Gardens https://longwoodgardens.org/blog/2021-02-25/how-grow-early-spring-vegeta-bles#:~:text=If%20timed%20carefully%2C%20the%20vegetable,crops%20like%20tomatoes%20or%20peppers.
- Crop Rotation in the Vegetable Garden https://yardandgarden.extension.iastate.edu/how-to/crop-rotation-vegetable-garden
- 10 Ways Cover Crops Enhance Soil Health - SARE https://www.sare.org/publications/cover-crops/ecosystem-services/10-ways-cover-crops-enhance-soil-health/
- The impact of NPK fertilizer on growth and nutrients.. https://www.ncbi.nlm.nih.gov/pmc/articles/PMC8794100/

- 10 Simple Ways to Amend Soil https://migardener.com/blogs/blog/10-simple-ways-to-amend-soil?srsltid=AfmBOoqOi52CmUZ0yxKg05qWD3uMsK5LZPJdH5b8yXFsvEPJLxUmotSP
- Essential Nutrients for Plants | Texas A&M AgriLife Extension ... https://agrilifeextension.tamu.edu/library/gardening/essential-nutrients-for-plants/
- 8 Methods of Composting https://directcompostsolutions.com/8-methods-compos-ing/?srsltid=AfmBOoqM3lkCBItSOABB8dXvB1ARcYwVPMNJDtXyP3ghbZvqIYgmHvI7
- Companion Planting: The Ultimate Guide for Pest Control ... https://ezfloinjection.com/article/companion-planting-the-ultimate-guide/
- 8 Natural Insecticides That Won't Harm the Earth https://www.treehugger.com/natural-homemade-insecticides-save-your-garden-without-killing-earth-4858819
- Attracting Beneficial Insects https://extension.psu.edu/attracting-beneficial-insects
- How to Lay Out a Companion Planting Vegetable Garden https://www.thespruce.com/companion-planting-vegetable-garden-layout-8639173#:~:text=The%20available%20space%20and%20light,much%20shade%20during%20the%20day

- Small Space Vegetable Gardening Tips https://www.thespruce.com/vegetable-gardening-in-small-spaces-1403451
- Best Vegetables to Grow in Pots (12 Great Container. https://www.foodgardenlife.com/learn/best-vegetables-pots
- The Biggest Basil and Tomato Companion Planting Benefits https://foodgardening.mequoda.com/daily/vegetable-gardening/the-biggest-basil-and-tomato-companion-planting-benefits/
- 9 Tips for Successful Raised Garden Bed Gardening https://www.vegogarden.com/blogs/academy/9-tips-for-successful-raised-garden-bed-gardening
- How to Build a Greenhouse in 8 Steps https://lawnlove.com/blog/how-to-build-greenhouse/
- 7 Advantages to Greenhouse Gardening https://roostandroot.com/blog/7-advantages-to-greenhouse-gardening/
- How to Build a Hoop House for Garden https://www.almanac.com/how-to-build-hoop-house
- Maintaining Your Hoop House Greenhouse - Boot-strap Farmer https://www.bootstrapfarmer.com/blogs/building-a-greenhouse/maintaining-your-hoop-house-greenhouse
- Deep Water Culture (DWC) Systems: A Complete Guide for ... https://ponicslife.com/deep-water-culture-dwc-systems-a-complete-guide-for-hobbyists/

- **Nutrient Film Technique (NFT):** A Complete System Guide https://ponicslife.com/nutrient-film-technique-nft-a-complete-system-guide/
- A Recipe for Hydroponic Success - hort.cornell.edu http://hort.cornell.edu/greenhouse/crops/factsheets/hydroponic-recipes.pdf
- 12 Hydroponic problems and how to solve them https://ourlittlesuburbanfarmhouse.com/12-hydroponic-problems-and-how-to-solve-them/
- 9 Best Dwarf Fruit Trees to Grow in Small Spaces https://www.bhg.com/best-dwarf-fruit-trees-7107205
- How to Prune Dwarf Fruit Trees https://www.finegardening.com/project-guides/pruning/how-to-prune-dwarf-fruit-trees
- 10 Best Berries to Grow in Your Garden This Spring https://www.thepioneerwoman.com/home-lifestyle/gardening/g42695071/best-berries-to-grow/
- Blueberry Care Guide: How to plant, grow, and ... https://www.monrovia.com/be-inspired/blueberry-care-guide.html
- 10 Versatile Culinary Herbs to Include in Your Garden https://theecologycenter.org/10-versatile-culinary-herbs-to-include-in-your-garden/
- Rosemary Plant Care Guide: How to Grow This Herb Indoors ... https://www.marthastewart.com/rosemary-plant-care-8640647

- Growing, Harvesting, and Preserving Herbs https://extension.psu.edu/growing-harvesting-and-preserving-herbs
- Your Guide to Growing, Drying, and Storing Herbs and ... https://www.consumerreports.org/home-garden/gardening-landscaping/your-guide-to-growing-drying-and-storing-herbs-and-spices-a4049277287/?srsltid=AfmBOook3ZG_fZrm4VW9mwLUeoTotTJgvWmpsHf9O-q5arHqGCvyXGOH
- The Top 18 Chicken Breeds for Your Backyard Flock https://homesteadandchill.com/backyard-chickens-top-18-breeds/
- How to Build a Chicken Coop: The Definitive Guide https://www.almanac.com/raising-chickens-101-how-build-chicken-coop
- Rhode Island Red vs. Buff Orpington: Which Chicken Breed Is ... https://poultrymanual.com/rhode-island-red-vs-buff-orpington/
- Where to Buy Chicks and Chickens (Online + Local) https://dontwastethecrumbs.com/where-to-buy-chicks-and-chickens/
- Where to Buy Heirloom Seeds: https://rootsandrefuge.com/where-to-buy-heirloom-seeds/
- How To Read A Seed Packet - Denver Urban Gardens https://dug.org/how-to-read-a-seed-pack-et/#:~:text=The%20front%20of%20your%20seed,of%20what%20you're%20growing!

- Seed Storage and Handling - USU Extension https://extension.usu.edu/vegetableguide/production/seed-storage-handling
- The Value and Significance of Saving Seeds and How it ... https://www.permaculturenews.org/2015/05/11/the-value-and-significance-of-saving-seeds-and-how-it-benefits-you/
- How to Build a Compost Bin: Step-by-Step Guide with Photos https://homesteadandchill.com/how-to-build-a-compost-bin-tutorial/
- How to Make a DIY Compost Bin: 13 Easy Builds for Beginners https://lawnlove.com/blog/diy-compost-bin/
- 5 Benefits of Using Cold Frames In Your Garden https://redemptionpermaculture.com/5-benefits-of-using-cold-frames-in-your-garden/
- The Keep It Simple Guide To Cloches http://nwedible.com/the-keep-it-simple-guide-to-cloches/
- A Step-by-Step Guide to Water Bath Canning https://www.alphafoodie.com/a-step-by-step-guide-to-water-bath-canning-for-beginners/
- Pressure Canning Safety: 10 Rules to Live By https://foodgardening.mequoda.com/daily/food-preservation/pressure-canning-safety-rules-to-live-by/
- How to Freeze Fresh Fruits and Vegetables https://www.eatingwell.com/article/15848/how-to-freeze-16-fruits-and-vegetables/

- How to Use a Food Dehydrator https://www.allrecipes.com/article/how-to-use-a-food-dehydrator/
- Dirt Cheap: 12 Easy Ways to Garden on a Budget https://zerowastehomestead.com/dirt-cheap-12-easy-ways-to-garden-on-a-budget/
- 20+ Beautiful Garden Crafts to Make with Recycled Materials https://www.creativegreenliving.com/2017/04/20-beautiful-recycled-garden-crafts-to-make.html
- DIY Natural Fertilizers & Homemade Pesticides For Your Garden https://healthy-indian.com/lifestyle/gardening/diy-natural-fertilizers-homemade-pesticides-for-your-garden/
- Dirt Cheap: 12 Easy Ways to Garden on a Budget https://zerowastehomestead.com/dirt-cheap-12-easy-ways-to-garden-on-a-budget/
- Permaculture for Small Gardens - GrowVeg.com https://www.growveg.com/guides/permaculture-for-small-gar-dens/#:~:text=Three%20permaculture%20principles%20%E2%80%93%20'Integrate%20rather,designing%20your%20small%20permaculture%20garden.
- Zero Waste Gardening. The Ultimate Guide. - Living Green https://livinggreen.uk/thethriftyecogardener/zero-waste-gardening-the-ultimate-guide

- Permaculture Design For Small Spaces | Maximizing Yield ... https://www.ecolife.zone/permaculture-design-for-small-spaces
- 27 Upcycling ideas for the garden that look amazing https://www.idealhome.co.uk/garden/garden-ideas/upcycling-ideas-for-the-garden-273290
- Find a local gardening group / RHS https://www.rhs.org.uk/get-involved/community-gardening/find-a-group
- Public Health Benefits of Community Gardens https://publichealth.tulane.edu/blog/benefits-of-community-gardens/
- 10 Online Gardening Communities You Should Join https://www.treehugger.com/online-gardening-communities-you-should-join-4858500
- Let's Talk Gardens Webinar Series https://gardens.si.edu/learn/lets-talk-gardens/

We'd Love Your Feedback!

Thank you for reading **Backyard Farming**. We hope you found it insightful and valuable.

If you enjoyed the book, we would be incredibly grateful if you could take a moment to leave a review on Amazon. Your feedback not only helps other readers discover the book — it also supports our work and makes a big difference.

Simply scan the QR code below or visit the link to share your thoughts.

Or visit:
www.amazon.com/review/create review?asin=B0F7XYKS3N

Or visit our website:
https://synastbooks.com

With heartfelt thanks,
CODY TRENT

www.ingramcontent.com/pod-product-compliance
Lightning Source LLC
Chambersburg PA
CBHW061824040426
42447CB00012B/2807